21 Ways to Build Your Teenager's Self-Esteem

♥

Susan Barton & Katherine Ingram

ANNE O'DONOVAN

First published in 1995 by
Anne O'Donovan Pty Ltd
171 La Trobe Street Melbourne 3000

Design and illustrations by Lynn Twelftree
Cover design by Parkhouse
Cover photo of authors by Ponch Hawkes
Typeset by J&M Typesetting Services
Printed by Australian Print Group, Maryborough

Cataloguing-in-publication entry

Barton, Susan
    21 Ways to build your teenager's self-esteem

    ISBN 0 908476 80 9.

    1. Parent and teenager. 2. Self-esteem in adolescents. 3.
    Self-perception in adolescence. I. Ingram, Katherine. II. Title.
    III. Title: Twenty one ways to build your teenager's self-esteem

    158.1

Publisher's note: Every effort has been made to source
quotations and request permissions but the Publisher
would be pleased to hear from anyone who has not been
acknowledged.

Phone numbers and details in the Resource File were
correct at the time of going to press.

The Lighthouse Foundation

The Lighthouse Foundation is a not-for-profit, private foundation based in Melbourne, aimed at preventing homelessness for young people by providing long term accommodation in a family home, together with the love, nurturing and family life that is every child's right.

The Lighthouse Foundation was established by Susan Barton who, for the last 15 years, has cared for up to 13 children at the one time. Susan's success rate with young people in her care has been so high that there is now a demand to accommodate more children and to duplicate her system and loving care in other 'Lighthouses'.

Contents

Dedication

This book is lovingly dedicated to our greatest teachers, our children, Brett, Cooper, Chandima, Renee, Kane, LaToya, Ramesh, George, Jacob and Melanie, Cam, Richard and Anna, and all the other children who are so precious to us, who have touched our lives in ways that have blessed and enriched us.

Acknowledgments

To all the countless people who have supported us with love and inspiration and expanded our horizons, our heartfelt thanks.

Some of our teachers who have contributed to our kaleidoscope of experience over the years have been our mothers, June Layton and Jessie Ingram, who have also been our greatest fans, Carol Glover, Cynthia Johnson, Gurumayi, Shanti Gowans, Leila Thompson and Jane Jordan.

This book was made possible because of the loving support of our friends Terrie Barton, Michael Laffy, Val and Jim Byth and Edwin Adamson.

Who are we?

Susan has made her life's work looking after teenagers from dysfunctional backgrounds, teenagers whom most people have given up for lost. Kids who have lived on the streets, young offenders, physically, emotionally and sexually abused young human beings. Kids who are truculent, aggressive, acting out anti-social behaviour of every variety and often not at all attractive to be around. What is obvious from Susan's experience with these young people is that is is never too late to start learning how to live life more productively and joyously, whatever your past history.

A couple of years ago, we decided to write a book about the work that Susan was doing with the Lighthouse teenagers and their inspiring stories of courage and hope. We wanted to document constructive ways that Susan was using to build real relationships with some of these teenagers, who were in the 'too hard basket' for most other people in their lives.

Katherine has long been interested in holistic ways of living and began to write down what Susan was doing intuitively.

Much of what we were documenting were traditional ways where relationships, connectedness and community were more important than structures and authority.

For the last year we have both lived with the Lighthouse family, of a dozen or so young people, including some of Susan's own children. Another half dozen or so come for meals, meetings and visits, and generally hang out as part of the extended family, although they don't actually live there.

We have developed a strong commitment, which Lighthouse has adopted, to

the journey	**rather than**	the destination
the means	**rather than**	the end
how we do things	**rather than**	what we want to achieve
the process	**rather than**	the product
who are we becoming	**rather than**	who we will be or were

The systems and procedures that we use at Lighthouse are based on the following:

Inclusivity All members of the family share the right to be included in all the decision-making processes that concern them.

Conflict resolution We assume that all conflict is resolvable. We aim to find win/win solutions to problems, so that all parties are happy with the solution.

Dissent and questioning are encouraged. Learning to ask good questions is encouraged, because we believe this is a way of seeking good information.

A high degree of truth is required from all members of the family.

Agreements We ask that people only make agreements that they intend to keep and complete.

Understanding is emphasised and attempts are made to understand the *whole* person.

Responsibility We expect people to be fully responsible for themselves and for their actions. Family members are encouraged to continue working to become the best that they can be, no matter what their age or status. We are all learning.

Connectedness Family members are encouraged to concentrate on what we have in common, rather than what makes us different or divides us. They are encouraged to develop a feeling of belonging to the family and to develop a feeling of connectedness to all people and their environment, our beloved planet.

Relationships are more important than rules, and most rules are negotiable.

Empowerment We seek to empower family members to take control over and have responsibility for their own lives.

Family Meetings are a forum in which young people are encouraged to express themselves, listen to others and respect the rights of others. Openness, trust and an ability to express contentious issues honestly and clearly can be developed. Negotiation skills are encouraged. These meetings are meant to be involving, encouraging and good fun most of the time.

Introduction

We believe that good parenting is a matter of acquiring good skills as much as being a loving human being. Those skills can be learnt, though it is not always easy to find someone to learn from. And once you have acquired some strategies, you need to put them into practice. Hone your skills.

We both feel that our own children have been our greatest teachers. Looking back we realise that some of our worst moments with teenagers turned out to be when we learnt the most, and we can now laugh at the way we were hooked into some of their dramas. But because of these situations, we set about learning a range of skills that have equipped us to deal better with the dramas that a household of a dozen or so lively young people provides.

Living with teenagers certainly accelerates your own growth so you might as well make the most of it and learn as much as you can.

We have both been committed to learning life's lessons as fast as we could, and have had many experiences of complex, difficult circumstances dissolving once we learnt some simple skills. We both study in many different ways as much as we can about the human condition and we find it more and more fascinating as we go. Our journeys have taken us on courses and seminars, fire-walking, abseiling, through books and films and academic study. It has developed within us a sense of keen observation, of trust for our own intuition and experience.

We have both had considerable stints as single mothers on fairly limited incomes. Both of us have struggled along as well as we could but with a fair degree of anxiety at times, having no real role models for what we were doing, and not knowing how it was all going to turn out.

We have used our hindsight and our daily living with the kids around us to put this book together. On reflection, we both agree that when we most needed some of these techniques we often did not think to use them. Practising them when things are going smoothly ensures that when you hit the rough patches, they are more likely to emerge naturally as effective responses.

There are many well-documented challenges that the coming generations will have to face.

How can we prepare teenagers for change happening faster than we can imagine its consequences? We need to explore, to develop responsibility and creativity in the next generation. We believe that high self-esteem will certainly help teenagers face these challenges.

High self-esteem is about liking yourself and feeling good about yourself. It is a prerequisite for trusting and acting on your intuition, for continuing to develop your creativity, and for valuing others and their ideas along with your own.

When your self-esteem is high you don't have to win at all costs; you can be flexible when you need to be. You are your own person. You can behave spontaneously and don't have to constantly measure

yourself against other people's star
responsibility for fulfilling your d
accept your feelings and can recogni
happy and angry and fearful and s
safe enough to express your feelings appropriately.
Your life is likely to be full and rich with satisfying,
happy relationships. You are effective and productive.
And we need lots more people like you!

Low self-esteem means that you have your eye on
someone else to assess how you are going according to
their values. You have to prove yourself all the time,
prove that you are right, and therefore that others are
wrong; or you are unaware that you have something
of value to offer the world, you don't believe in yourself and you lack the confidence to really enjoy life.

Young people need to be encouraged to dream
bigger dreams, to design their own dreams and to
hold the vision of their dreams. What do they *really*
want to do? Who do they want to be? What do they
want for the world? How are they going to integrate
what they want for themselves with what they want
for the world?

We knock all hope out of young people when we
let them believe that succeeding at school is the only
way they will ever get anywhere. By encouraging
them to believe this, we forget that it is the journey
that counts not the destination, and that there are
many ways to a happy, successful life.

Your teenagers don't have to succeed in all the
areas where you would have liked success. Sometimes
you have to honour the fact that their path is different
from what you would have chosen for them. Just

...member to focus on the person with all the love and positive attention you can, rather than on the behaviour.

We suggest you use this book as a resource – we hope that you might learn something from what we have learned. It is designed to help parents feel *more* adequate. It's crucial for parents to have high self-esteem too. Most parents do a great job and all do the best they can at the time. We are certainly not Superwomen and we know we couldn't have done it without very good friends and family. And we're still on the journey. We're still learning ...

As a parent your self-esteem is inextricably linked to your children's self-esteem.

10 Ways to start building teenagers' self-esteem

Listen to your teenagers

Hear what they say

Spend time with them

Share something with them

Laugh with them

Hug them

Help them see the positive side of life

Encourage them to try something new

Trust their inner wisdom

Focus on their best qualities

Children have never been very good at listening to their elders, but they have never failed to imitate them.

James Baldwin

1 Demonstrate

*B*e the role model you choose to be, because your children will do as you do rather than as you say every time.

Listen to your teenagers. Listening is by far the most important thing you can do for any relationship. All too often we want to jump in and tell our story or give solutions. This often breaks the rapport. Listen with the intention of understanding. Listen with your eyes and your heart. If you *really* listen to your kids, and try to hear what they're saying, there is much more chance that they will listen to you.

Have something in your life that adds value to the world, thus modelling for your children a wider view of the world. You and your teenagers might join an environmental group, such as the Wilderness Society or Greenpeace or Global Energy Network International or Friends of the Earth; or get involved in tree-planting in the local area.

Take your teenagers' concerns for the environment seriously. Implement suggestions of theirs for a more environmentally friendly household. Ask them to be in charge if it is something they feel strongly about.

Take an interest in what their interests are. But wait to be invited to contribute. Don't be tempted to take over and tell them how they could do it better.

Show them the value of inner strength, co-operation, self-discipline, diligence, intuition.

Never doubt that a small group of thoughtful, committed people can change the world. Indeed, it is the only thing that ever has.

Margaret Mead

Embrace challenges Problems are opportunities for creative problem-solving. They are what make you strong, add interest to life. At the same time, don't take on everything as a personal challenge.

Stretch out of your comfort zone and expand your notions of what is comfortable. When you are too comfortable, it is time to do something else.

Show your teenagers that there is no need to be afraid

of conflict. It is only an opportunity to practise creative solutions and negotiation skills.

Read inspiring books. Borrow inspiring videos. Watch inspiring films with the family and them discuss.

▶▶▶ **Focus on what works.**

Keep them informed about your life decisions — the good as well as the bad — so that they can learn to make good choices for themselves.

Become community minded. Encourage your local council and school to implement some real activities for young people, such as leadership training.

Show your children the value of planning and organisation, as well as spontaneity.

Beauty is truth, truth beauty —
that is all
Ye know on earth, and all ye need to know.

John Keats *Ode on a Grecian urn*

2

Tell the truth: it's simpler, wastes less time and energy

*B*e sincere in your exchanges with young people. Tell them only the truth, simply. Resist any urges to show off your wit, cleverness or humour at their expense, particularly when you see an opening that is really funny.

Have simple, sensible conversations with them, sharing yourself with them to the extent you feel comfortable.

Respect their privacy Young people need to be able to trust you not to read their diaries or listen to their phone calls. They need to know that their boundaries are respected.

Connect them to other stimulating, caring, capable, wise adults and let them know that they can turn to these people if they need to, at times when they don't want to confide in you. Choose these adults with them at a non-crisis time, and speak to those concerned, letting them know what you have decided.

Encourage the expression of a *wide* variety of feelings in your family. Being true to yourself involves knowing who you are and how you *really* feel.

Show your teenagers how to express their feelings without causing harm to anyone, themselves included, or blaming others for 'causing' bad feelings. For example, 'You make me mad' gives someone else the power to control their moods. 'I feel mad when you do that because it interferes with what I am doing' gives the other person information and the speaker takes the responsibility for feeling mad.

The quality of the journey is decided by the amount of truth you are telling to yourself at any one moment.

Talking to kids who feel that life is futile

Some young people feel at times that life is futile, that there seems no hope for themselves, or for the world, and that no one seems to care or do anything. And it wouldn't matter if they did. It's too late to clean up the mess anyway. It often seems to be the most creative, sensitive and intelligent teenagers who feel this way.

Listen carefully to how they feel Acknowledge that is how they feel at the time and that you understand their feelings. It's useless giving them false assurances. In fact, it's a wonder that more people do not feel that way more of the time.

So many of us experience a sense of separateness rather than a sense of connectedness with ourselves, our family, our tribe, our place in the greater scheme of things. A vague feeling of loss can come with this separateness. Because we do not know what the loss is about we cannot even acknowledge it. Connecting with your true purpose for being here can help overcome a feeling of futility. If teenagers are aware that there is a point to being here, they are more likely to find it. They may not even know exactly what their purpose is, but we believe that when people experience feelings of joy and peace about what they are doing, the more likely they are to recognise a purpose in their lives.

When they feel less depressed, ask them to suggest some steps they could personally take to try to make a difference; to work as a volunteer for an organisation such as Greenpeace, or an organisation devoted to social justice.

Be on the lookout for inspiring life stories so that you can tell them to dispirited youngsters, when the time is appropriate. Learn the stories of people such as Nelson Mandela, the South African President who appointed as his Vice-President the man who had put

A great teacher once said,

'We cannot direct the wind but we can adjust our sails.'

♥

him in gaol for twenty-seven years; or Rigoberta Menchu, a Guatamalean peasant women who has become a powerful peace activist and winner of the Nobel Peace Prize, despite witnessing members of her family being tortured and killed by the military.

There is cause for concern about our survival and that of our planet, and it is up to each individual to make his or her own contribution. That is the message that you need to get across.

*Life is either a daring adventure
or nothing.*

Helen Keller

Have fun with your teenager

3

Make sure you have fun together. For every stern moment, make sure you have at least one good laugh together. However, don't try to force them to laugh.

Enjoy your children as people. Go with them to things they enjoy. Watch TV shows that they choose. Sit with them. Massage their backs.

Let them take an occasional day off from school to do something special with you. Create a really special day, planning and talking about it together being a major component. Make the most of it so that it will become a wonderful memory.

Remind the kids that you were once a child, even a teenager. Behave like a kid sometimes. Relax, loosen up, muck around.

Go camping. Join the Youth Hostels Association. Go sailing or skiing.

Have adventures. Plan them in detail together.

What does it mean to be happy? Some call happiness a feeling of satisfaction, comfort, fulfilment and inner peace. Others refer to joy, excitement and communion. The sensation of happiness might be unique to each of us; however, we know when we're there. We can note certain common characteristics. When we're happy with ourselves, we are accepting of ourselves (not judging ourselves). When we're happy with others, we're accepting of them (not judging others). Happiness brings us closer together rather than pushing us apart. But above all, happiness makes love tangible. To love someone fully and completely is to be happy with that person, to accept him without judgments and celebrate his existence. To love ourselves it to be happy with who and what we are, to accept ourselves without judgments and celebrate our own existence.

Barry Neil Kaufman

Learn to roller blade with your children.

Teach your teenagers to entertain their friends at home, several at a time from an early age, so that when they go to larger parties they won't have to feel socially incompetent or get drunk to cover their shyness.

Include them in as many adult social activities as you can and demonstrate acceptable behaviour.

Go out as a family.

Go for a night hike in a National Park with a ranger who will show you the night-life. Have a moonlight picnic.

Go out for a hot chocolate or coffee together, sometimes with one teenager at a time, just to be together.

Go to your teenagers' sporting events and concerts. And not just school events: take in an occasional basket ball game or pop concert. Just because they are old enough to go by themselves, don't miss out by not going along. And who knows? You might have a good time.

Swim with dolphins.

Build sand castles.

Hire a convertible and take a drive along the coast.

Row on a river. Paddle a canoe to a picnic spot.

Whatever you can do or dream you can,
begin it. Boldness has genius, power
and magic in it.

Goethe

4 Encourage your teenager to dream

There are two types of dreams: sleeping dreams and dreams of what might be. Both are valuable and it's worth encouraging your teenagers to think about their dreams.

Encourage your teenagers to dream bigger dreams and to extend their dreams. What are your children's dreams for themselves and their world?

Help your teenagers to understand that those 'dreams' can become goals, and those goals can become reality.

At the Lighthouse, an important part of what is offered to those who come to live there is to identify their dreams, no matter how impossible they seem.

Subscribe to a really good environmental magazine such as *Earthwatch* or *National Geographic*. Or borrow them regularly from the local library. What dreams can unfold by learning to love the world around us?

The Senoi people, who live in the mountainous jungles of Malaysia, are reported to be extraordinarily well-adjusted psychologically and to show remarkable emotional maturity. They live co-operatively, peacefully and creatively. It has been suggested that 'their use of dreams is a basic element in developing these characteristics.

When Senoi children first begin to report dreams, their descriptions are very much like dreams of all children, in which, for example, frightening animals or monsters chase them. By the time they are adolescents, they have eliminated nightmares and consistently produce creative products from their dreams ...'

The first rule to accomplishing the remarkable change in their dream patterns is 'to confront and conquer danger' in dreams.

The second rule is to 'advance towards pleasure in a dream', to relax and enjoy the pleasurable sensations of flying, for instance.

The third rule is to 'achieve a positive outcome ... The ultimate positive outcome ... is a [beautiful or useful] gift to the dreamer from one of the dream images ... to share with family, friends, and the tribe in general.'

Patricia Garfield

Sleeping Dreams

Ask your teenagers about their sleeping dreams. Encourage them to keep a dream journal and to tell the stories of their dreams in detail: first person, present tense and with the colours, smells and feelings related to them vividly recorded.

Ask your children how they interpret their dreams. Is there a message for them? Is there something they could paint, draw, make, write about or sing?

Discuss dreams in the morning when they are fresh. For most people, young and old, their own dreams are a fascinating subject of discussion and exploration.

Nothing in the world can take the place of persistence. Talent will not; nothing is more common than unsuccessful men with talent. Genius will not; unrewarded genius is almost a proverb. Education alone will not; the world is full of educated derelicts. Persistence and determination alone are omnipotent.

Calvin Coolidge

5 Help your teenager to set goals

*A*chieving goals is an excellent way of building self-esteem. It can help teenagers understand that they can indeed take control of their lives and it can provide a tremendous boost to their confidence.

Talk to your teenagers about what they would really like out of life, exactly what their goals are. They may have quite short term goals but they may also surprise you by their grander long term goals.

Encourage them to set goals, to write them down and to focus on them. Encourage them to work towards those goals — both big and small.

When setting goals, they need to be very clear, and the best goals are SMART:

1. **S**pecific
2. **M**easurable
3. **A**chievable
4. **R**ealistic, and have a
5. **T**ime frame for them

Encourage your teenager to set goals for:

The Big Dream
Career
Community contribution. How can they help others
or contribute to the community?
Global dreams
Health and fitness
Hobbies
Places they want to go
Relationships with family and friends
Savings and money
School
What they want to be good at
What they want to improve on
What they want to learn about

 And while you're at it,
what about your own goals?

New Year's Eve is a good time to review goals. Revise
them at least each quarter — solstices (midsummer
and midwinter) and equinoxes (when day and night
are of equal length in autumn and spring), lend themselves to this sort of activity. Check on your goals
monthly and weekly.

What do you need to do to correct and get back on
target? When Apollo 11 was heading to the moon with
the first astronauts on board, it was on target 3% of
the time. So you don't have to be on target all the time.
You just have to be prepared to keep monitoring your
progress and keep making the necessary corrections.

Affirmations are powerful, positive statements, expressing the way you would like your life to be. They can support goals very powerfully. They will be stronger and more effective if they are in the present and include the person's name. Help your teenagers make up their own affirmations.

I,	I,	I,
.............,	.............,	.............,
now study with enthusiasm all that I need to know to pass with flying colours	*now run 1500 metres with ease and grace*	*now support my body by looking after it – eating the right food, exercising with enjoyment and sleeping soundly*

Your teenagers, and you, will find it helps to do more than just visualise your goals. Why not create a collage of what you wish to achieve? Set aside an evening to gather around with magazines, glossy brochures, cards, scissors and large sheets of paper or folders. The idea is for everyone to cut out pictures that depict what they are aiming for and create a collage of what their goals might be: a happy family, a healthy body, a new bedroom, a successful career, places they'd love to travel to, or whatever.

Stick positive affirmations all over the house.

Passion
always
persuades

Anita Roddick

What you
FOCUS
on
you get

I approach
new challenges
with enthusiasm

I am
happy and relaxed
about
my accomplishments

You can add words, or affirmations or descriptions —
anything you like really. Then each person adds his or
her photo to the collage. This cut-and-paste activity is
great fun, and really does help you visualise your goal.

When setting goals, we always ask that 'the good of all concerned be considered in the attaining of these goals'.

Sometimes we become attached to what we think is a great goal and we attempt to force the outcome. If we can set the goal clearly and release any attachment to having it, we allow space for a bigger picture to come in to play.

Suggest your teenager finds a mentor, whom they can relate to. They could also talk to successful people and ask them about their goals and how important goals were to them along the way.

Encourage young people to be realistic and at the same time to set goals that stretch them. It is not only about achieving them. It is also about what happens along the way, who they become in striving for goals.

Help them to observe the side-effects of going for their goals, the journey towards the goal, what inner strengths they develop as they go. What could not have happened if they had not set the goal?

Talk about what life might look like when they are twenty? Thirty? Sixty? What will they be doing? Have done? Who will they be?

Celebrate achieved goals and decide how you are going to do that when you set them.

▶▶▶ **Celebrate having a go!**

*There is nothing wrong with mistakes.
I've made more mistakes than anyone
I know. That's why I know so much.*

Buckminster Fuller

Teach your teenager ...

... that anything can be resolved. Nothing is insoluble. Some things may take a little longer than others. And sometimes life is just plain unfair. When things seem unfair, what lessons can be learnt?

... negotiation skills. Negotiate, negotiate, negotiate.

... responsibility. Teaching young people to be responsible for their actions and circumstances is a key strategy at Lighthouse. We see this as crucial. If they never properly learn to take responsibility for their actions, they remain powerless victims with no control over their lives. This often means *you* have to step back and let your teenagers experience the consequences of their actions.

... to know the difference between excellence and perfection. And then encourage them to strive for excellence. The difference is worth learning. You can drive yourself and everyone around you crazy being hooked on perfectionism. It can mean that you discourage yourself and everyone else from having a go

10 more simple ways to build teenagers' self-esteem

Let yourself love them just the way they are

Respect your teenagers' privacy

Listen with all your heart

Be there Don't withdraw if there's a problem

Laugh at their jokes (at least sometimes!)

Be consistent

Acknowledge them whenever you can

Honour their individuality

Create a happy home

Enjoy your *own* life

at something because you are frightened of not doing it perfectly. Excellence on the other hand, is worth striving for. Let others assess their own degree of excellence and encourage them to do their very best, better than last time, and to complete tasks rather than leave them unfinished.

... that mistakes are wonderful learning experiences. The more they make, the faster they'll learn. Asking questions furthers this learning. Guard against your own need to be seen as a 'perfect parent' if it interferes with your teenagers learning.

... to save some of their pocket money. 10% should go into an investment account that they never touch. 10% can go into an account to save for things they want. And it's a good idea to encourage them to give 10% away to something worthwhile.

... to learn to talk to their inner child. Their inner child has a wealth of information for them and reconnects them with their vitality, trust, work effectiveness, job and life fulfilment.

... that their feelings are their friends. A knot in the gut can give them a valuable message that something is wrong. Tension in the shoulders may be trying to tell them something.

... to learn to listen to their intuition and to trust it enough to take action sometimes. We have found that the more we have acted on our intuition, the more connected with our intuition we have become.

… to enjoy intellectually stimulating ideas. Encourage them to expand their ideas.

… to keep asking questions — from everyone they want to learn from. No question that stems from a genuine desire to learn is ever too dumb or unimportant to ask.

… to question assumptions, to appreciate paradoxes.

… to be discriminating (and then don't be surprised if they use that faculty differently from how you expect).

We learn wisdom from failure, much more than from success.

Samuel Smiles

Empowering adolescents

Help your children develop skills and tools that enable them to make informed choices by:

  allowing them to experience the consequences of their actions

  participating in personal development workshops, where a wide variety of skills and tools, such as goal-setting, communicating team building, telling the truth, taking responsibility and negotiating, are taught.

  being open and honest about yourself

  listening to them empathically

  having a circle of funny, loving and interesting friends and family of which they are a valued member

Having a variety of good role models around for young people helps them to establish meanings and values, ideals and goals and, eventually, their own personal standards.

Ultimately unbounded awareness (allows) you to realise that you are the field of all possibilities, that you have the ability to create anything. It's really that you are the magician behind the trick, that you are the creator behind the creation ... To know that you have to expand your awareness.

Deepak Chopra

7 Take a creative approach

*I*ntroduce your teenagers to meditation and try it yourself if you have not already done so. This is probably the most important thing that both you and your teenagers can start practising.

Visit some of the bigger yoga centres when they have a special meditation event, such as an all night chant.

Brainstorm solutions and ideas with your teenager, or with the whole family, if there is a problem to resolve or a challenge to confront.

Brainstorm creative options. Suspend judgement when you do this. Even the most bizarre idea is written down with the rest. All ideas are great ideas. Judgement at this stage inhibits the wilder, more creative ideas from flowing. Brainstorming is about quantity first. How many ideas can you find? Quality comes later. What's the best combination of options?

Trust young people's intuition and wisdom and teach them to explore, strengthen and value these inner resources.

We've found that teenagers often have the best solution to their own challenges, if they are given the opportunity and the tools to discover the answer.

Ask your teenagers for their ideas in important family matters, for example, moving house, or a family holiday. Let them feel they have a valued input into the household, and therefore they truly become a valued member of it.

Encourage them to do the opposite of what they would normally do sometimes, especially if it means facing a fear. For instance, if they're afraid of heights, would they try abseiling with a skilled instructor?

Introduce them to people, television programs, videos, films, magazines that present creative solutions to the world's challenges.

Leave notes in their school lunches and under their pillow telling them how wonderful you think they are and why. Write love letters to your children. If it was your last day on earth, what would you like them to know about the depth of your love for them?

En-**courage** young people. That means to give them courage. Courage is making a commitment to take action, despite doubts that they may have.

▶ ▶ ▶ **Support them to do what they need to do. Don't do it for them, but give them all the encouragement they need.**

Acknowledge your teenagers at every opportunity, especially when they have great ideas, when they are doing well. And look for the things they are doing well. Focus on the positive things. Give them lots of attention then.

Go star gazing. Find the nearest telescope when something exciting is happening in the heavens. Study astronomy.

Play charades.

Let them take time out to dream. Wonderful creative ideas often come quietly. You sometimes have to listen carefully or you miss them.

Spend time in the library together.

The real voyage of discovery consists not in seeking new landscapes, but in having new eyes.

Marcel Proust

Dream of harmony. Lighten up.
Take some fresh air and sunlight.
Work for peace.
Sacrifice for love.
Make a wish.
Look through the eyes of appreciation.
Make someone happy.
Never be disheartened.
Do not wait for a better world.
Accept love.
Ring an old friend.
Write poetry.
Giggle.
Be still.
Respect the Earth.
Dance with the stars.
Expect the best.
Be silly.
Sing.
Follow your bliss.
Hug a tree.
Practise random acts of kindness.
Kiss a child.

Author unknown

Read a book in a tree.

Give them a book — not only for a birthday, but just to remind them that you do think about them.

Encourage them to build cubby-houses. Susan's children were still building cubbies when they were 16 and 17 years old, and some teenagers get great satisfaction from helping younger kids to build cubby houses.

Cuddle up with your adolescents and read them fairy stories by firelight. There have been some beautiful books written about the importance and significance of fairy tales and myths. You could choose a child's book of fairy tales that they remember from their younger years. Or something like the stories in *Women Who Run with the Wolves* by Clarissa Pinkola Estés. No matter how old you may feel, particularly if this isn't what you are used to, give it a go, because the kids (after the initial wariness) love it.

Paint and draw with the hand you use least and encourage them to try to do it too.

Have concerts. Print programs. Have rehearsals. Invite other members of the wider family for dinner and the concert.

There is nothing more potent than thought. Deed follows word and word follows thought. The word is the result of a mighty thought, and where the thought is mighty and pure the result is always mighty and pure.

Mahatma Gandhi

Learn massage together.

Encourage them to give each other massages, especially after an upset. The person who causes the upset owes the upset person a massage when they feel less angry.

Collect your family stories. Tape a series of interviews with the oldest members of the family. What were their favourite games? What did they do on holidays? Who was their favourite grown-up? What subject did they like best at school? Ask them to tell stories about any old photographs you or they have. These stories should really be attached to the photos. Build on the family store-house of memories. Interview more widely. Contact family members you don't know. This encourages friendships with other people who may have much to share.

Tell your teenagers positive, and funny, family stories often.

Encourage your teenagers to keep a diary and to write their own family history through their eyes.

*I always taught my childcare staff
that we are in the business
of creating memories.*

Carlene De Tres

8 *Establish rituals*

*D*evelop family rituals and traditions that build trust, rapport and stability. These can serve as anchors and keep families together.

For some, family may mean friends that you consider your family.

Remember — you are building memories that your children will carry into adulthood and pass on to their children.

Celebrate everything — winning, having a go, birthdays, anniversaries, religious festivals whether they are your own or other cultures', midwinter, midsummer, successes, progress, completions. When you celebrate them regularly, they become rituals that the whole family can look forward to.

Emphasise the celebration and the fun and games, not the present-giving or any expensive element. Plan the celebrations together. Invite friends. Choose special foods and decorations. Combine with other families for these celebrations and share the planning and the work.

Include the whole family in as many family occasions, weddings, funerals, festivities, as possible. Help them to develop a sense of their place in the wider family tribe.

Develop family rituals around at least one meal a week, and saying, 'Good morning' and 'Goodnight' every day.

10 Real life tips from teenagers
(What teenagers would like ...)

To **talk** with parents on an equal basis

To **have** clear boundaries

To be **acknowledged** for the good things they do

To **know** they're loved

To **be** listened to

To **be** treated as though they are *wanted* by their parents

To **be** believed in

To **have** parents believe in them

To **be** included

To **have** parents 'lighten up' around them

The family unit is where children learn to resolve the tensions between individual rights and the common good. The mistake we made post-sixties and through the seventies was to think that the social unit was the individual ... We are herd animals. I'm all in favour of this swing back to the family ... I do keep saying

we have to pay more attention to each other

or we're going to be in serious trouble in terms of our sense of community and, by implication, our sense of morality.

Hugh Mackay

9 Hold family meetings

*F*amily meetings are an important way of creating and encouraging confident young people, who are able to express themselves, listen to others and respect the rights of others. They are a process for developing conflict resolution and creative problem-solving skills. They develop solution-oriented, responsible adults rather than powerless victims.

When young people have input into how the life of the household is organised, they will really support you because they own the decisions. They will often make sure themselves that the agreements are kept, so that you have the whole weight of peer pressure behind you.

Self-esteem develops with these skills and experiences. Knowing that their opinion is as important as anyone else's enables young people to accord the same value to others' opinions and points of view.

These meetings help young people to see the difference between the person and the behaviour, and develop openness, trust and an ability to express contentious issues honestly and clearly.

The Five Freedoms

1. *The freedom to see and hear what is here, instead of what should be, was, or will be.*
2. *The freedom to say what you feel and think instead of what you 'should'.*
3. *The freedom to feel what you feel instead of what you 'ought' to feel.*
4. *The freedom to aks for what you want, instead of always waiting for permission.*
5. *The freedom to take risks on my own behalf, instead of choosing to be only 'secure' and not rocking the boat.*

Virginia Satir

The meetings should be involving, encouraging and fun. When the participants see things happen as a result of decisions made jointly, their self-esteem rockets up.

Don't just have a meeting when there is a problem. Regular family meetings can promote harmony.

The Lighthouse family has a meeting once a fortnight and only in extreme cases are excuses for not attending okay. For example, if there is a speech night or a graduation. The commitment to the meetings is important.

Both our families have experienced much improved communication among young people after family meetings, and discussion can continue well into the evening after the meeting has finished. There is often a sense of lightness and joy because the unexpressed baggage that people have been carrying with them has been aired.

Such meetings also form the basis for trust and communication later in their lives. Some of the young people who have moved out of Lighthouse to live independently continue the meeting forum. So we guess that speaks for itself.

Topics discussed can include:

- the needs of individuals
- complaints, although don't let them become whinge sessions

- family outings
- up and coming events
- the chore roster for the week with logical consequences to follow when chores aren't done
- contingency plans in case someone is unable to do their chore
- acknowledgments of good experiences
- establishing guidelines

How to run a meeting

Set up a structure. Agree on the time and place convenient to everyone. Establish an agreement that everyone will attend, or under what circumstances the meeting will go ahead if everyone isn't present.

Negotiate rules of the meeting with the whole family. A good one to start with is only one person speaks at a time. This also encourages listening skills.

Take turns in the chair. The role of the person in the chair is to make sure that all points of view are heard and that people focus on the issues under discussion. Encourage round table discussion, everyone having a say.

Allow all to have their say with as little adult interruption as possible. We have found that when the meetings have been held consistently, that the chairperson can handle all issues. However, occasionally a parent may need to step in, take control and set reasonable limits. This can show that the parent cares about the whole family, if handled appropriately. It doesn't need to be seen as a take-over and cause resentment.

The meeting is the place to discuss and establish the Rules of the House, so that everyone is clear what they are, and why they *are* rules.

Let them make mistakes and develop their own style.

Rotate the position of note-taker. Keep notes, particularly of the agreements, and keep them accessible so that people can refer to them easily if and when necessary.

A good rule is that when people have complaints they need to be able to present at least two possible solutions. Encourage them to become creative about solutions. This switches the focus from the problem to the solution and helps teenagers to develop habits of solution orientation.

Consider alternatives: 'How else could we do this?'

Build win/win solutions. Make sure you reach resolution, not compromise. Learn the difference. You need to let go of wanting to force a particular outcome if

One man awake
Can awaken another.
The second can awaken his
next-door brother.
The three awake can rouse the town,
By turning the whole place upside down.
And the many awake, make such a fuss,
They finally awaken the rest of us.
One man up with the dawn in his
eyes - multiplies.

Helen Kromer

you are going for win/win. Something bigger and better than anyone could have come up with on their own often emerges as a true win/win solution.

When you reach a compromise, someone is disappointed.

Do your best to understand your teenagers' needs and concerns, and help them to communicate these needs and concerns.

Close on positives. Each person says at least one positive thing about one other person. For example, 'Thank you ... for helping me with my homework chores last Tuesday', or 'I think you're very courageous giving up smoking. Good on you.'

It is not fair to ask of others what you are not willing to do yourself.

Eleanor Roosevelt

10 *Set reasonable boundaries*

Establish reasonable boundaries sooner rather than later, while everyone is still calm.

Talk about the big issues such as drugs and alcohol before they become a problem and establish boundaries early on so that your teenagers know what is acceptable.

Develop boundaries using the guidelines you have negotiated at family meetings. They may differ for individuals according to age or maturity. Refer to the non-negotiable Rules of the House when necessary. (See *Family Meetings*.)

Teach teenagers that they are accountable by allowing them to experience the logical consequences of their actions.

We have found that it sometimes helps to draw up a contract, with those concerned, that they agree to and sign. Explore what the logical consequences of acting outside the boundaries may be, such as removal of privileges.

The consequence is not a 'punishment'. It needs to relate to what the person has done. For example, if your teenager has lost yet another term travel concession card, he or she may have to walk to school until the end of term; or perhaps contribute to paying for a new one.

If an agreement is broken they cannot argue about the consequences. It takes the onus off you to be the enforcer all the time.

Make as little fuss as possible about things that you don't like but that don't really matter. Ask yourself what is really important. Exploring new things is part of being a teenager. A passing fashion fad can be aesthetically displeasing but rarely dangerous.

Check your own behaviour. Are you setting a good enough example?

Let teenagers know very clearly that you are not going to tolerate outrageous behaviour connected with such things as drugs or alcohol. That you are prepared to help them find somewhere else to live, if necessary, as a last resort. Do they need to stay at a relative's house for a couple of weeks? Often adolescents behave more outrageously at home than elsewhere, and they can often be quite charming with other people. (A book worth reading on this subject is *ToughLove*, listed in the *Resource File*).

Let them know that when they are ready to behave differently, you are very willing to continue living with them, or whatever it is that continues your relationship with them.

Understand that boundaries are about unacceptable behaviour and not about the person. Help them to distinguish their behaviour from themselves.

If you think the problem is getting out of your control, you may need support from someone trained to help you develop a strategy and stick to it. (See *Resource File*.)

Continue your own education. Learn Transactional Analysis, Parent Effectiveness Training (P.E.T.), Neuro Linguistic Programming (N.L.P.) or some other framework that enables you to quickly analyse interactions, particularly repetitive ones that become patterns.

Stay in touch with other parents and be aware of the boundaries set for your teenagers' peers. You may not agree with them, but at least be aware of the peer group pressure on your own teenagers.

Make sure your expectations are realistic.

Some parents expect their kids to be everything *they* were — or everything they *weren't*. Or they expect them to *do* everything they did or everything they *didn't*. Trying to live up to these unrealistic expectations can destroy a teenager's self-esteem. Losing sight of your teenagers' individuality can stifle their creativity and their ability to do all sorts of wonderful things you have not even imagined.

Remember always to look for the positive. Acknowledge your teenagers when they do accept and live within the boundaries agreed upon.

Never feel that you *have* to justify your decisions or behaviour, although you may choose to explain your reasons.

It's not about what they have done, or not done, that matters, but what they are going to do about it ... and how fast!

10 Things that work for our families

Listening to each other

Brainstorming until we reach resolution

Giving love unconditionally — with no strings attached

Teaching teenagers to find their own answers

Trusting that teenagers *can* find their own answers

Making time to spend together

Affirming our love frequently

Letting go of always having to be right

Telling the truth

Loving ourselves, so we can love others

It is the heart that does the work.

Listen to the heart.

*It will tell you truly where you live.
When you turn to your heart,
which the Light has filled to overflowing,
you may know the joy of the Soul.*

John-Roger

Look behind the anger

11

*H*ow parents deal with their own and their children's anger is crucial.

Anger is a fact of life, a natural emotion. It usually comes after another feeling or emotion — fear, frustration, resentment, fatigue, worry, guilt and embarrassment are just some of the possible causes. Try to look beyond *your* anger to see the real cause — and help your teenagers look for the cause of their own anger.

Our children trigger unresolved feelings from our own childhood. Our reactions are therefore often out of proportion to the actual incident we are facing. Review what was happening in your own life when you were the same age. Have your feelings of inadequacy been triggered? Did your parents put you down? Don't be surprised if you need help with this one.

Repressing the anger may only push it below the surface. Expressing the anger physically may be temporary solution — and a good one if it doesn't harm anyone. But looking for the original reason and talking it through can often resolve the problem.

Take yourself off to a room with a baseball bat or a tennis racquet and vent your rage on pillows and cushions. Play a recording of Tchaikowsky's *1812 Overture* and have a good yell as the cannon blasts off. Dance energetically. Sing at the top of your voice when you need to. This may syphon off anger that belongs to *your* past, not the present, and enable you to deal with the present much more clearly.

Teach your children to handle their own anger appropriately. Get them a punching bag. It's not OK for them to take it out on brothers, sisters, yourself or the furniture. Allow them to get rid of their anger energetically. It's useless talking to a child who is full of rage. Teach them to take 'time out' when necessary.

Encourage teenagers to stay fit. A gymnasium membership may be worthwhile and also give them a safe place to get rid of frustration and anger.

Often writing a letter to a person you are feeling angry towards will help, even if you decide not to send it. Just being able to express your sadness or frustration helps get rid of the anger.

Help your children to recognise that feelings are okay. It's okay to be angry. But encourage them to look at what really made them angry. What can they do about it? And how can you support them to do something about it.

After an angry incident has defused, it's possible to talk about it and work out ways to handle similar incidents in the future. How can they recognise when their feelings are getting out of control? What bodily reactions do they notice? What triggers it?

Learn to give 'I' statements and teach them to do likewise. Instead of saying 'Turn that music down or else...' try saying 'I feel miserable and uncared for when you do that...' Describe the behaviour. This gives the other person some quality feedback. State the tangible effect. Name your feeling. This reduces blaming and shows them how to take responsibility for their own feelings.

Teach them that crying or losing their tempers or laughing or ignoring something are only some of the possibilities that they can choose to respond to other people's behaviour.

People are always blaming their circumstances for what they are.

I don't believe in circumstances.

The people who get on in this world are the people who get up and look for the circumstances they want, and if they can't find them, make them.

George Bernard Shaw

Defusing Situations

Handle emotions calmly. That's all they are — emotions. They don't signal the end of the world.

E – motion

=

energy in motion

By just acknowledging the particular emotion and naming it, such as: 'You're really angry', you could be surprised at how quickly this simple statement can begin to establish a calmer frame of mind. This is called reflective listening and it is a very useful skill to develop.

De-escalate. Undermatch. If your teenager is furious at force ten, counter with force eight or nine, not force eleven, twelve or twenty-five.

Be flexible. Negotiation's the way to go, not rigidity.

When children want to do something new, 'trust' is irrelevant. Trust is knowing how they will behave rather than believing that they will always 'do the right thing'.

Trust is built on past experiences and enables you to predict how they will behave in particular circumstances. They have to demonstrate how they behave in those particular circumstances, maybe a number of times, first.

Laughing and crying are often very closely related. While you do not want to trivialise their need to cry by making them laugh inappropriately, sometimes interrupting the direction of a volatile situation by introducing an absurd element can be effective.

Remove yourself until you are calm enough to deal with the situation. Walking is very healing. Go for a long walk until things are back into perspective for you. Ask yourself what is important. Your need to win and be right OR your relationship with the person provoking the upset?

Step into the other person's shoes and try their reality on for size. How would you have reacted at their age? What answer would you have wanted?

Mackay's 10 Commandments of Communication

1 It's not what our message does to the listener, but what the listener does with our message that determines our success as communicators.

2 Listeners generally interpret messages in ways which make them feel comfortable and secure.

3 When people's attitudes are attacked head-on, they are likely to defend those attitudes and, in the process, reinforce them.

4 People pay most attention to messages which are relevant to their own circumstances and point of view.

5 People who feel insecure in a relationship are unlikely to be good listeners.

6 People are more likely to listen to us if we listen to them.

7 People are more likely to change in response to a combination of new experience and communication than in response to communication alone.

8 People are more likely to support a change which affects them if they are consulted before the change is made.

9 The message in what is said will be interpreted in the light of how, when, where and by whom it is said.

10 Lack of self-knowledge and an unwillingness to resolve our own internal conflicts make it harder for us to communicate with other people.

Hugh Mackay Why don't people listen?

To see your drama clearly
is to be liberated from it.

Ken Keyes, Jr

12 *Side-step dramas*

Most families will experience challenges around anger, sex, drugs, alcohol, smoking or eating disorders at some stage. In fact, one or more of these subjects is pretty well guaranteed to create some dramatic upsets.

Like most things, dramas are a matter of degree. What for some will be a flash-fire, for others will seem totally devastating. Find ways to keep your perspective and balance.

Look at worse scenarios occasionally. Consider 'what is the worst that could happen in this situation?'

Reflect on your own youth.

Maintain your sense of humour.

Have courage: face problems honestly. Don't ignore them hoping they will go away.

Remember that often things aren't as bad as they seem.

Keep your eye on the big picture, the longer time frame during these times, while at the same time, dealing as practically as possible with the circumstances at hand.

Support your teenagers. And remember that if the problem is serious you too need support — from friends, from family and from professionals. (Check out the *Resource File* at the end of the book — and follow up some of the contacts.)

Treat serious issues seriously. If you are so 'tolerant' and 'cool' that you are determined not to notice outrageous or destructive behaviour, your young people may well stage bigger and bigger dramas until you take some notice. So learn to stay calm and firm, without denying that attention is needed.

Remember that the teenage years are a time for teenagers to experiment, explore boundaries and establish their own identities. We would worry if our children were so passive, submissive or unadventurous that they did not develop minds of their own. However, it is often a surprise to realise that, after years of encouraging children to make independent decisions and to take responsibility for them, that their decisions are very different from what we might have expected.

In many cases, where there are major problems they may be indications of wider family problems.

Look at your own life.

Are *you* angry and resentful?

Are you and your partner in conflict?

Are you trying to control your teenagers too much?

Do you give them enough responsibility?

Are your young people feeling that they have little or no control over their own lives?

Are they bored?

Do they feel that a sure-fire way to get attention is to cause an upset about something controversial?

Is it really as alarming as you think it is?

Can you negotiate more reasonable boundaries?

Sometimes dramas are truly of soap opera proportions, but not always. It is worth practising on the little dramas. Learn to recognise the patterns. How do they start?

Teach young people how to recognise and to ask for what they want in a straightforward way: a hug, some quality time and attention. If the answer is to be 'No', help them to work out a satisfactory alternative. Teach them to be able to accept 'No' graciously when necessary. It does not mean that they are unlovable.

Learn to separate the person from the behaviour. We can't emphasise this enough.

Loving the person and not accepting unacceptable behaviour under any circumstances, no matter how dramatic, and allowing teenagers to give appropriate vent to their feelings, are crucial to managing these situations creatively.

Encourage teenagers to fulfil their need for drama in properly taught, skilled activities such as acting, music, abseiling, rock-climbing, parachuting, hang-gliding, firewalking, white water rafting, netball, football or tennis rather than creating family soap operas. All these activities are excellent in building self-esteem, your own as well as theirs.

Teach teenagers to distinguish (and learn to distinguish yourself) between surface drama and what may be going on underneath.

When they are telling you how unfair something is, how totally powerless they are in some situation, ask them 'What would the other person concerned be saying or thinking right now about the situation?' Use this question gently. Don't be tempted to bully them. Help them to realise that there are other points of view.

Give your attention to positive behaviour. Focus on what you want to increase and expand. Learn to be very ho-hum about negative behaviour and dramas that are not really serious.

Resist the urge to give into bullying behaviour from teenagers as a 'treat', 'just this once then'.

Do not be threatened by the possibility of a major upset. Learn to see upsets as opportunities for creative problem-solving.

Separate 'treats' from contentious issues. Make them unconditional, not if they do something that you want them to do.

Practise getting to the core of what is upsetting **you**. Ask yourself if there is something frightening for **you** in the situation. Are you finding if difficult to acknowledge their independence? Do you feel a need to control their values, attitudes and beliefs? Can you cope with difference?

The most important thing for you to do if your teenager is creating ongoing, destructive dramas involving drugs, anorexia, bulimia or truancy, to name a few possibilities, is to build your skill level with expert help.

When some misfortune threatens, consider seriously and deliberately what is the very worst that could possibly happen.
Having looked at this possibility with real conviction, 'Well, after all, that would not matter so very much,' you will find that your worry diminishes to quite an extraordinary extent. It may be necessary to repeat the process a few times, but in the end, if you have shirked nothing in facing the worst possible issue, you will find that your worry disappears altogether and is replaced by a kind of exhilaration.

Bertrand Russell

Major dramas

▶▶▶ Drugs, eating disorders, truancy, criminal activities or worse ...

You discover that your adolescent is experimenting with drugs. Or you suspect a serious eating disorder. Or you learn of criminal activities. What do you do? The emotional needs underlying these behaviours can be huge. Peer pressure can play a significant role too. We have found that the higher a younger person's self-esteem, the more likely they are to make constructive choices for themselves.

Stay calm — don't panic, no matter how dramatic the circumstances.

Get professional help.

You need to develop and strengthen your own skills, to keep communicating effectively. Check all the resources you have available to you, including similar resources to the ones at the back of this book.

Keep loving your teenagers. Focus on the underlying needs for love and attention.

Don't waste time trying to blame someone — or anyone.

Common sense is not so common.

Voltaire

Don't panic! Smoking, alcohol & other drugs

We use substance abuse (smoking, alcohol, other drugs) as examples of behaviour that most parents find alarming, but there are many self-destructive behaviours. The same methods of empowering yourself to deal squarely with the challenges apply to anorexia, truancy, criminal activities, and other situations which can be truly frightening.

Smoking

If adults around them set the pattern and smoke, young people are likely to smoke — often long after the adults have stopped.

Children start smoking sometimes out of curiosity, sometimes because they get the message that it's okay, that it's socially acceptable. There is pressure for young people to drink and smoke to fit in with their peers, to look cool, to experiment. Advertisers portray sexual, sensual lifestyles attained by smokers and drinkers.

People, young or otherwise, will only stop smoking when it is a problem to them. They have to know that stopping will benefit them.

Lead by example. Don't expect them to give up if you don't! Demonstrate how you deal with social awkwardness, stress, boredom, nervousness, anxiety, good and bad feelings without a cigarette.

Set up appropriate guidelines for you and what works in your home. Decide if the house is to be tobacco-free? Does this mean that they can smoke outside? If so, that means that no matter how wet and cold, smoking happens outside. Fullstop. No discussion.

Educate them: leave material around about the health problems related to smoking — cancer, emphysema, coughing, reduced circulation, pregnancy problems, premature ageing, gangrene. But, we hate to tell you, this is likely to have very little effect one way or the other.

Place the responsibility for stopping into their hands — but give them all the help you can when they decide they are ready to stop.

When your children decide to give up smoking provide support, understanding and encouragement. Encourage them to have a plan — to cut down, to avoid places where they know not smoking will be difficult, to hang out with non-smokers, to drink plenty of water to clear the nicotine from their system and to exercise. Suggest that they save up for something special with the money that they will save. Have a monitoring system for watching the money grow, such as pinning the dollar bills on a bulletin board. Sometimes it can take several attempts to give up. Remember that each attempt is a step in the right direction.

Alcohol

What can we say here? Alcohol presents just as many problems and the potential for just as much drama as other drugs do. The major difference is that there are many parents setting a daily example of how to use — and often abuse — alcohol.

▶▶ **Alcohol is socially acceptable in most circles, but it is still a drug.**

If you do drink, remember the example you are setting and avoid using it as a crutch to help with problems. Your teenagers will recognise this and are likely to follow suit when they hit a rough patch.

'Binge drinking' — the 'drink-til-you-drop' style of consumption, is just as dangerous as continuous and regular consumption of alcohol. Any heavy drinking is particularly dangerous for teenagers whose livers are not yet fully formed. If your teenagers are coming home drunk, talk to them (when they are sober, of

The best thing about the future,
is that it comes only one day at a time.

Abraham Lincoln

course). Don't start by reading them the riot act. Find out if they are trying 'to drown their sorrows', or succumbing to peer group pressure.

Forbidding them to drink at all is not the way to go. Instead, hand over the responsibility to them. Let them know that you trust them to drink in a responsible way.

This is when you need to be very clear about the guidelines that you have all established for the household. (See the section on setting reasonable boundaries).

Finally, if you want a drug-free home, it's worth considering if you are prepared to forgo prescription drugs, tobacco and alcohol yourself.

Other drugs

Teenagers take drugs to enhance the way they feel about themselves and the world around them. They may be trying to cover feelings of inadequacy, the strain of coping with pressures to achieve, unhappiness at home, unhappy selves, unhappy relationships, unemployment and peer pressure. One reason they keep going back to drugs is that the effect is instant. Instant gratification. Instant relief from boredom. Instant relief from pain within.

Many adolescents use butein gas, glues and aerosols instead of pills, marijuana and heroin.

Compared to harder drugs, marijuana is considered by some people to be a 'soft' drug because it does not have the stigma attached to it that speed and heroin do.

Most of the time you can recognise when adolescents are on drugs because there are many changes in their habits. Not sleeping, not getting up, not wanting to eat, having the munchies, mood swings, dropping out of sport and schooling interests, not caring and the inevitable trouble that follows.

Kids have to realise and admit that they have a problem before anything can be done.

Do not panic! Smoking dope does not mean that they are junkies. Many teenagers experiment with dope and will never be addicted. Some will experiment with other drugs and come to no harm.

Let your teenagers know that you love them and have time for them. Let them know that no matter what happens, you will always be prepared to help them the best way you can.

This does not mean paying their debts or fines and allowing them to escape the financial and legal consequences of taking drugs. Spend money on them in other ways; for example, by going away for the weekend with them or by taking them out for dinner to talk — and *listen* — somewhere quiet away from home.

Keep communication channels open without making judgements. You will probably need help to be, and stay, non-judgmental if the circumstances seem to be out of control.

Educate yourself about drugs and their effects. **Seek the best advice and support possible**. Know what is available before you need it. Get support for yourself through groups such as Assertive Parenting, Tough Love, Al Anon or Nar Anon. See the *Resource File* at the end of the book for a few suggestions and then check what is available to you locally.

For teenagers, there are Twelve Step programs such as AA, Al Teen or Nar Anon. There are also other programs that have a different perspective. All of these are worth exploring.

But it is totally useless trying to drive your children to any of these if they are not absolutely willing to go. You only buy into very sophisticated game-playing, rescuing, persecuting and being a victim in terrible cycles. Far better to get the support that *you* need.

Understand that you are a role model and so are your friends. If you smoke, misuse prescription drugs or alcohol, then chances are that so will your children.

If your children have problems and admit to them, celebrate. This is the first step along the way. If they go into a detoxification centre for only a short time at first, celebrate, knowing that they have come this far.

Know thyself

Delphic Oracle

14 *Be honest about sex*

Sex is a wonderful and important part of a loving partnership. It is important to make sure teenagers know this. Modelling a loving, caring, affectionate, playful, responsible, committed, intimate relationship for them is the best way for them to get the message.

If this is not altogether possible, provide good role models for them from among your circle of family and friends. Or from books and films. Discuss relationships in videos and films that you watch. Are they realistic? Convincing? What would have happened if … she had walked away? … he had listened to what was being said? How could the tragedy have been avoided?

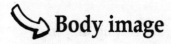 ## Body image

Teach them to love their bodies. This means looking after them.

How to get your teenagers to love their bodies and treat them well, without becoming obsessed by them, is another question. There are the extremes of obesity and anorexia, teenagers who seem loathe to move a muscle and those who are willing to spend endless hours in a gym and take steroids to change their body shape.

Either of these extremes, and many of the variations in between, can be signs of low self-esteem.

Acknowledge that your teenagers may be feeling anxious about their changing shape. We all went through it, but is doesn't make it any easier for the next generation. Don't dismiss their concerns.

Have a look first at your own attitude to your own body. Are you setting a good example? Do you slump in front of the television with a few tinnies or a packet of chocolate biscuits? Do you get enough exercise and eat a reasonable amount of healthy food? Do you starve-diet and then binge?

It's often just as important for parents to remind themselves that every *body* is different and that there are all types of bodies.

Try not to pressure your kids into feeling they *have* to look a certain way. And though its hard to convince them that narrow shoulders or wide hips are genetic, it's at least worth trying. Take a look at the rest of the family, or the extended family, and you're sure to see some family characteristics.

Encourage your teenagers to become involved in some sort of regular exercise or sport. By example, teach them to appreciate their bodies.

One of the best books we've seen on body image is *Real Gorgeous* by Kaz Cooke. It's a well-balanced book that tackles 'the truth about body and beauty'. It's recommended for 'women from 11 to 111', an amusing read, that should make even teenage girls laugh. We hope there is something similar on the way for boys and men.

Young women need access to medical advice with which they can feel comfortable. They need to know about breast self-examination, and Pap smears.

Celebrate your daughters' first menstrual periods. Encourage them to see them as an exciting step forward. Read up on the ancient rites of womanhood and share them with your daughters. Encourage them to observe their rhythms and cycles closely and to notice if there is any connection with the moon's cycles. Encourage them to listen to their bodies and to see if they can feel when they are ovulating.

Relationships are not outside — they are inside us; this is the simple truth that we must recognize and accept.

My true relationship is my relationship with myself — all others are simply mirrors of it.

As I learn to love myself, I automatically receive the love and appreciation from others that I desire. If I am committed to myself and to the truth, I will attract others with equal commitment.

My willingness to be intimate with my own deep feelings creates the space for intimacy with another. Enjoying my own company allows me to have fun with whomever I'm with. And feeling the aliveness and power of the universe flowing through me creates a life of passionate feeling and fulfilment that I share with anyone with whom I'm involved.

Shakti Gawain

Be aware that young people can be very sexually active. Be aware of your own experiences, past information, values and attitudes. Discuss with teenagers how your beliefs have affected your own behaviour.

Keep checking your own feelings and attitudes to your children's sexuality. Are you fearful? If so, what is the fear about? Are you scared of unwanted pregnancies? Homosexuality? Sexually transmitted diseases?

If you are uncomfortable about raising these subjects with your children, work out what is making you so. Perhaps you are afraid of them growing up. Make sure they do have someone they can speak to, or confide in, apart from their peer group.

Have you religious beliefs that mean it would be difficult for you to accept them experimenting with sex?

No amount of threatening or dire warnings will stop them. But such warnings often do affect how responsible they will be about contraception and safe sex. Very often children from religious homes will take awful risks with sex rather than admit even to themselves that they are sexually active. They would prefer to think that they were carried away on the spur of the moment rather than take any premeditated responsibility for making a decision.

If you disagree with them having a sexually active relationship, be truly clear with yourself what your objections are. But be prepared for their decisions to be different from what you would choose for them. How will you respond if they don't take your advice. Are you then going to damage your relationship with them long-term? Turn them out of the house? Or are you going to negotiate as honestly as you can, letting them know what your fears are?

Educate yourself. Keep yourself up-to-date with such issues as safe sex and AIDS. Latex condoms have been proven to be the most effective prevention against AIDS/HIV infection. It is a good idea for adolescents to know how to use them properly. Buy some for them to practise putting them on a couple of their fingers — girls as well as boys.

How do your sons feel about young women carrying condoms? Do they think this means that they are 'asking for it'? How do your daughters feel about carrying condoms? Do they feel confident about negotiating the use of them? They may as well know that world-wide, many older, more experienced women do not seem to be very successful at such negotiations.

However, if your teenagers are not ready to talk to their partners about safe sex, are they ready to be sexually active? It's a question worth asking them.

Be open. **Resist the urge to dictate**. Discuss with them, and in their presence, issues such as AIDS/HIV; the use of condoms; abortions and what you can do and where you can go to have one; or how to continue with the pregnancy; the Pill and other contraceptives;

responsible sex; homosexuality; being in a caring relationship; age and readiness for a sexual relationship. There are plenty of good books and videos available for both you and them to explore.

Make sure they know where good advice and information is available. Take them to explore the libraries at Family Planning Centres or clinics set up to counsel young people about contraception and abortion.

Make sure they know that abstinence is one very distinct alternative to intercourse. And that the safest ways to have sex are non-penetrative options to intercourse. Activities such as hugging, massage and mutual masturbation can all be options worth considering.

If parents are secretive, children will go elsewhere for information. The best way to address sexual behaviour is to thoroughly inform them and to let them know that there is nothing they cannot tell you if they need to. Tell them, 'Whatever you decide about sex, make sure you play it safe'.

Keep the door open for more and more complex conversations about sexual relationships. Check in occasionally by making reference to something in the news or in a film and asking for their opinions. They will definitely not express an opinion if they think it is just a sneaky way to get information out of them, or if they think that they are going to be judged for it — even silently!

We have known situations where young people will not go to their parents when they are in some kind of trouble because they have 'too good' a relationship with them and do not wish to 'disappoint' them.

It is very important to keep the doors open for communication.

It is very important for young people to know that they can say 'No' to sexual advances at any stage, even halfway through. And to know that they should develop their intuition and trust their feelings when something does not feel right.

Discuss negotiation skills. Does anyone near you run courses teaching them? Negotiation skills are very useful tools for young people to have in their own personal tool-box.

Both of us have had more to do with sexual abuse than we would have liked. However, we have found that the most empowering action you can take for a child is to treat it seriously, be prepared to make an appointment with a police woman from, say, the Rape Squad, if necessary. You can ring them first and discuss with them the best way to go about this. You may choose to confront the offender and to give the young person the chance to tell them that it was not okay for them to do what they did, however long ago.

Seek the best possible advice from a variety of sources before you make a move.

No Secrets People who work with abused children say time and time again it's the shame that secrecy causes that does the long-term damage. Let young people know there's nothing they can't tell you. You'll have to cope with listening without being shocked or judgmental.

Young people often begin a conversation leading to the revelation of sexual abuse with something like, 'If I tell you something, will you **promise** not to tell anyone?'

We have both replied to this, 'I can't promise to do that but I will promise to consult you before I tell anyone else'. This is where **no secrets** is important because secrets only perpetuate the offender's protection and disempower the offended-against.

In the situations that we have dealt with, the clearest honesty has proved to be the best policy. However, consult widely first and make sure you get the best advice available to you. It can be heartening to discover just how much support there is out there in the community.

Learn to mourn.

This is a life-time of good-byes. As the years go on, you'll be saying good-bye to both people (through moving, change or death) and things (youth, that semi-tight body you once had, hair, prized possessions, etc.). Eventually you'll say good-bye to it all with your death.

Learning to mourn, to grieve, to say a good good-bye, is an invaluable tool.

When a loss takes place, the mind, body and emotions go through a process of healing as natural and as miraculous as the healing of a physical injury. Know that feeling lost, sad, angry, hurt, fearful and tearful at good-byes is a natural part of that healing process.

John-Roger & Peter McWilliams

15

Be sympathetic: grief, trauma, abuse

Grieving can be associated with not only the death of a person. The death of a pet, the loss of a friend, a miscarriage, abortion, separation, divorce, moving away from a neighbourhood or leaving a school can all bring about a sense of great loss.

It is important to speak truthfully and with care about death, trauma, abuse and any other kind of loss.

It is important for you and your teenagers to go through all the necessary stages of grief.

Elisabeth Kubler-Ross is one very experienced person who has written very movingly about loss and grief. Borrow her books from the library.

Feelings of loss need sensitive acknowledgment. Don't be alarmed by passionate expressions of grief by young people. Probably the more passionate the better. Let them get it out as much as they possibly can.

*We are healed of suffering only by
experiencing it to the full.*

Marcel Proust

Let your teenagers know that mourning is part of life and that they may as well take every opportunity to do it well. We see no point at all in a stiff upper lip.

Grieving often shows up as anger and feelings of abandonment, so watch for these reactions, and certainly don't respond with anger.

Not flesh of my flesh
Nor bone of my bone
But still miraculously my own.
Never forget for a single minute
You didn't grow
under my heart — but in it.

Fleur Conkling Heylinger

16 Face the reality of adoption

*B*e open and honest and truthful about the events surrounding the adoption and your feelings.

Give every opportunity, keep every avenue open for your teenager to contact his or her natural parents if and when they need to.

Trust that the teenager will have the intuition to know when this contact is best.

Give the teenager an ongoing opportunity to talk about it. And make the effort to listen.

At some stage the child may need to deal with early feelings of abandonment. Make sure you know how to tap into some of the excellent support and professional counselling services that are available.

We have found that healing the 'inner child' has helped clear those early abandonment issues. See John Bradshaw's books. There are some very good inner

Come to the edge, he said,
They said: We are afraid
Come to the edge, he said.
They came,
He pushed them,
and they flew.

Guillaume Apollinaire

child workshops and counsellors. See the *Resource File* for some suggestions.

Keep in touch with the adoption agency for support. Some agencies have teenage groups who meet on an irregular basis.

If the child was adopted overseas, establish and maintain contact with other families and children from the same country. Go to restaurants and collect recipes from that country. Collect literature, art and artefacts, music and travel posters.

Find ways in which your child is similar to you in mannerisms, voice, ways of doing things, and point them out to include them in the belongingness of the family.

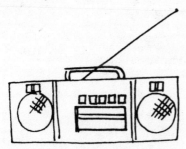

A child's life is like a piece of paper on which every passerby leaves a mark.

Ancient Chinese proverb

Accept that blended families are a way of life

*B*lended families are a way of life. In fact, they always have been. The myth of the happy mother, father and two point two children is a powerful image for us but the reality has always been something different. Not necessarily worse or better but definitely different.

So we don't have to continue to feel at odds with the world if we don't fit that stereotype. Many schools, for example, acknowledge different family constellations now. It might not always feel like it, but if yours is a blended family, you're in the majority.

A 1993 report by the Institute of Family Studies in Melbourne says that 'Australian parents today have something in common with their grandparents — about one sixth of them are bringing up their children on their own... the percentage of single parent families is now the same as it was 100 years ago. The rate has nearly doubled in the past 20 years, from 9.2 per cent

in 1974 to 16.6 per cent [in 1993]. The underlying causes of the rates of sole parenthood in the l990s and the
1890s, however, are fundamentally different.' (*The Age*,
30 August 1993.)

So families have always blended. Yet we sometimes
seem to cling to the powerful myth of what a family
should be and feel deprived if we don't have it. Now,
for all sorts of different reasons, parents are divorcing
and remarrying. This is creating a different sort of
blended family, with both parents alive and well, and
one of them often living not only with a different partner but with somebody else's kids. This obviously creates challenges and new sorts of sibling rivalries.

But affirming the rich and interesting side of blended
families means that each adult in a child's life can be a
kaleidoscope of experience and information. If the situation is handled well, children can have access to a
whole range of enriching support, value and substance. A variety of activities, holidays, people from
different cultures and countries can all contribute to
children's lives through blended families.

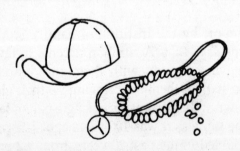

Step-siblings, half-brothers and sisters, step-parents, parents' partners, step-grandparents, ex-inlaws, grandparents' partners, step-parents-inlaw: all these can provide a very rich extended family, if that's the way you choose to see it. Aim to minimise the tensions and pettinesses, and to capitalise on the relationships involved. We have fractured enough extended families these days without depriving us and our children of the potential of these new types of extended families.

Encourage young people to see all aspects of their extended family as potential support.

You need never be threatened by your teenagers' relationships with other family members.

If all those in a parenting role undertook parenting courses the children's best interests would be more likely to be kept at heart.

If only one adult will undertake to do a parenting course that can make a very worthwhile contribution to defusing potential conflict. That adult can gain great support from the insights and the other participants in the course to defuse potential areas of conflict.

Children learn very early how to manipulate complex relationships between adults to get what they want, which is really love. If they don't feel that they get enough love they see other things as symbols for love. If one parent has more disposable income than the other, this can be source of heartache, jealousy and resentment. Or it can be something to work on and learn to put into perspective, for everyone's best interests. Money and what money can buy too easily become mistaken for symbols of love.

Create your own extended family. Adopt grandparents, aunts and uncles for your family if necessary – people who can share in your family's life and enrich it.

Understand that divorce does not mean you have ended the relationship with a co-parent. It has merely changed significantly. If you have children in common, you are in a sense related forever.

Live close by the other parent so that children are least affected by access arrangements. Encourage them to sometimes make their own arrangements with the other parent.

Encourage your children to have mentors whom they can trust and talk openly to, within this family network. A grandparent is often ideal in this role, but it might be an aunt or an uncle or a big brother or sister, maybe a newly acquired one.

Allow your children to experience living in different family environments if they express the need. It's not about who your teenagers love most. Often they want to stay with the non-custodial parent out of some misplaced sense of guilt. So it's good for them to go and work it out by experiencing the situation. They may have some need that they are not even quite aware of, that they find hard to articulate so don't make them over-explain their motives.

The ideal scenario for a child is to live in a trusting and safe group where they feel okay about expressing their feelings openly and know they are accepted for who they are. Families that can provide this know that children make mistakes and argue as part of the growing up process, but teach them to work together to resolve difficulties. They laugh together, show love and respect for each other and are probably good at listening.

What the mind does not know the eyes won't see.

♥

Deepak Chopra

Although love is always what we really want, we are often afraid of Love without consciously knowing it, and so we may act blind and deaf to Love's presence. Yet, as we help ourselves and each other let go of fear, we begin to experience a personal transformation. We start to see beyond our old reality as defined by the physical senses, and we enter a state of clarity in which we discover that all minds are joined, that we share a common Self, and that inner peace and Love are in fact all that are real. **Love, then, is letting go of fear.**

Gerald G. Jampolsky

Be responsible

Coping with your partner, other parents, non-custodial parents, step-parents

*N*ever let your children think that you have abdicated your authority over them to someone who isn't even their parent.

If your partner is not the other parent of your children, don't expect him or her to take over your parental role. Talk about it to see what you can expect.

It is very easy to be rational about other people's children. It's much more difficult, and not even desirable all the time, to be rational about your own. This means that you and your non-parent-of-your-children partner see things from a very different angle. That's fine.

You don't have to justify your position all the time. Develop confidence in the way you see your children, and be open to **quality** advice. Learn to tell the difference between quality advice and advice that comes from your partner's inner petulant child.

Seek help in negotiating these tricky waters if necessary.

Speak endearingly of the other parent's good qualities to your children, especially if they are showing similar qualities.

Avoid disparaging remarks framed as, 'You are just like your father/mother'.

There is not much you can do about your children's relationship with their other parent, whether or not you live together. That is for them to work out. If there is violence involved, however, whether physical or emotional, you will need to take action. The child will need help from the appropriate people. That means you and a very competent counsellor trained to handle domestic violence.

But give up trying to control your children's relationships if they are simply not much to your liking. If the other parent is prepared to participate in family negotiation sessions with a mediator, you are on to a good thing.

Compassion is the basis of all truthful relationship; it means being present with love — for ourselves and for all life ...

Ram Dass

Love is what we were born with.
Fear is what we learned here.
The spiritual journey is the
relinquishment, or unlearning, of fear
and the acceptance of love back into our
hearts. Love is the essential existential
fact. It is our ultimate reality and our
purpose on earth. To be consciously aware
of it, to experience love in ourselves and
others, is the meaning of life.

Marianne Williamson

Check your own world view

19

What do you really believe about life, love, the universe and everything? Our views are very coloured by our beliefs, experiences and how we see the world.

We believe that a higher force creates our world. We wonder at the miracle and mysteries of the human body and mind. And the human spirit we see every day in some of our young people particularly those who, from an early age, have survived treatment to which no human being should be subjected. We marvel at the beauty and wonder of the changing seasons, the awesome variety of Nature and we feel ourselves to be participants in the unfolding, eternal power of life. When the going was rough, these beliefs were the fundamental things that saw us through.

Unconditional love ...
that's what it's all about, really.

Unconditional love ...
it's a lifelong study.

*Miracles are in the everyday things,
the beauty of the trees that keep us alive,
reflections in a still river, rainbows over
the mountain top.*

*Prayer, to me, is learning to think with the
heart rather than the head. Thinking with
the heart gives a much broader,
wiser perspective on things.*

Susan Barton

Read widely so that you become clearer about what you really can believe in that will help you when you need it. Consciously develop a sense of clarity about your place in the universe and use these beliefs to help you through when the going gets rough.

In calmer times, we have listed everything that we have to be grateful for. We have both found gratitude to be a very productive state of mind.

We have both sought teachers who have demonstrated in their own lives an integrity that meant they practised what they believed. We have had different teachers at different stages of our lives and sometimes for different areas. Sometimes these have been professional counsellors, sometimes spiritual counsellors and sometimes friends who seemed to have it together a bit more than we did at that time. You do not feel so alone when you can tap into the wisdom of others. We have both given a high priority to facing the truth, accepting

Your children are not your children.
They are the sons and daughters of Life's
longing for itself.
They come through you but not from you,
and though they are with you yet they belong
not to you.
You may give them your love but not
your thoughts,
For they have their own thoughts.
You may house their bodies but not
their souls,
For their souls dwell in the house of tomorrow,
which you cannot visit, not even in your
dreams.
You may strive to be like them, but seek not to
make them like you.
For life goes not backward nor tarries with
yesterday.
You are the bows from which your children as
living arrows are sent forth.

Kahlil Gibran

responsibility for our circumstances and resolving as much as possible as often as possible — being prepared to rock the boat at times if it meant dealing with situations honestly.

Understand much of your teenager's negative behaviour in terms of them competing for your attention. **Positively beam quality attention, your total, undivided attention at your teenagers often, even if briefly sometimes.**

The more you focus on seeing the beauty of the person behind the behaviour and not the behaviour, the more attention you give this beauty silently or out loud, the more the behaviour will fall into line with it.

Practise this way of seeing your teenager before you go to sleep at night, when you're relaxed, before you decide to try it in the fray of the tantrum. Then practise it when they are in full flight, ranting and raving. Notice how quickly it can work. Be warned! You have to be feeling pretty mature and in control yourself to attempt this one. But it's worth working with because it can create magic.

Let your teenagers know you love them no matter what, but that some behaviours are not acceptable at all. Be clear about what they are.

▶▶ **Respect young people as individuals, not as extensions of yourself by whom the world will judge you.**

Have patience with all things, but chiefly have patience with yourself. Do not lose courage in considering your own imperfections, but instantly set about remedying them — every day begin the task anew

St Francis de Sales

Realise that they will have different views from you, as you probably did from your own parents, about social status, careers, partners, clothes, hairdos, tattoos, music and sexuality. Thank goodness!

Let go of any need to be right all the time. It's such a strain. Let go of any need to have to control or dominate.

Keep learning and challenging your most cherished beliefs.

Treat your children at least as well as you treat your best and most valued friend ... because that's what they can become.

Let you teenagers know that they are important not only to you, but to the planet. They have an important role to play in the future and it will mean being prepared to find new ways.

Rest is not idleness, and to lie sometimes on the grass under the trees on a summer's day, listening to the murmur of water, or watching the clouds float across the sky, is by no means a waste of time.

J. Lubbock

What you can do for you to get you through

You are your own best resource so take care of yourself.

Nourish and strengthen your own self-esteem and enrich your own inner resources. You can only give something of yourself to others if you *have* something to give.

Remind yourself that your own worth is never dependent upon what other people, even your children or your partner, are saying or doing. Keep your spirits up, no matter what.

Remember you can only ever love or be kind to someone else **nearly** as much as you love and are kind to yourself. Where does it come from otherwise? So keep working on loving and being kind to yourself — unconditionally. Be especially kind to yourself if your determination flags occasionally. Pick yourself up and

…to help get …ugh

Make sure you have a life of your own

Spend time with friends

Slow down

Take the time to be quiet

Ask for help, if you need it

Build your own self-esteem

Trust your own intuition

Look after your own health

Be kind to yourself

Enjoy your teenagers

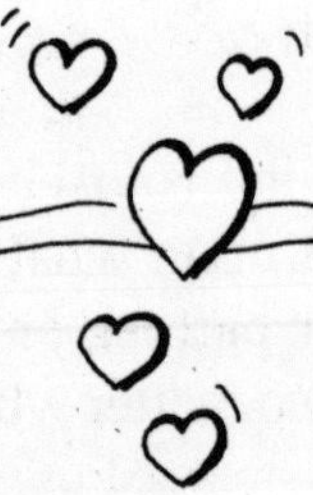

off you go again. Teach young people to accept and love themselves too.

Very few people feel loving and hopeful all the time. It's just that when we're feeling down, most of us are tempted to feel that it is a more permanent condition. We forget the more optimistic times. These feelings of confidence come and go. Aim to have more and more confident, happy times more and more often, regardless of what others in your orbit are doing.

Forgive yourself when you make mistakes, for not being perfect one hundred per cent of the time and for all the mistakes you have made in the past, even the ones you don't think deserve forgiveness. Mistakes are only opportunities to learn. Some lessons take longer to learn than others.

Parents aren't perfect. They just seem to think they have to be. So learn all the lessons you can from your children. They are your greatest teachers.

Remember you are a person first and a parent second. Recognise this and accept and respect yourself, your reactions, your feelings. This will allow you to accept and respect others' reactions and feelings better. Mutual respect grows out of being authentically who you are and allowing young people to develop the same authenticity. It often takes a bit of experimenting to get it right.

Take time to be quiet with yourself alone each day. Tune into the stillness. Consider meditating. And teach young people the value of the stillness — but not by making them be still!

Slow down every so often. Go away by yourself and just be.

Take time out to nurture yourself. Smell the roses, as the song says.

Choose a day occasionally to spend without speaking, not one word. You will be surprised at how liberating the experience can be.

Be loving to those around you. Explain beforehand what you are doing. Smile. Communicate in writing if you need to.

Stay in bed all day with a good book.

We've said if before but it's worth saying again. **Learn the difference between perfection and excellence.** Perfection is absolutely unattainable so give up trying. It paralyses you and prevents you from doing anything because you know that what you can do won't be perfect. Striving for the absolutely unattainable only creates chronic dissatisfaction, a very unattractive, unrewarding and frustrating condition.

Excellence means developing finer and finer skills. It means focus, concentration, commitment to doing the best you can and completing the task no matter what. It is about observing more and more closely what excellence in that particular field looks, smells, sounds, tastes and feels like.

We frail mortals are not perfect, none of us. So don't ever give yourself a hard time. Develop a sense of humour about yourself, without continually putting yourself down.

Take one high self-esteem producing behaviour and incorporate it into your daily life until it becomes second nature. For example, if you're always late make a commitment to be on time, and then keep that commitment.

Then pick another self-esteem producing behaviour and work on it. Note your progress. Sometimes it can take a year or two to break old habits and really integrate them into your repertoire of behaviours. So do it with some fun and be encouraged by all your attempts, even if they are not as polished as you would like them to be.

Be prepared to learn. Find a clutch of mentors who will guide you through the roughest patches. These could include someone like an older, more experienced parent: someone who practises what they preach, not someone who sets themselves up as an expert. These people are invaluable to you, so choose carefully. Very often, having the intention of finding such a mentor means that the very person appears. Know that when the student is ready the teacher appears. So observe closely. Sometimes teachers come in unlikely guises.

At different times of your life, different teachers and mentors will be relevant.

Surround yourself with people who stretch you, who ask more of you than you do of yourself. People who you know will tell you the truth.

Most people don't need solutions to problems or challenges, they just want to feel really listened to. We have found that most people have their own answers and will arrive at them if they are listened to with rapport.

Develop your active listening skills. Start conversations with:

> What do you think about ...?
> What was the most fascinating ...?
> What if ... something else happened/was happening?
> How could we do this differently?
> What's your opinion of ...

Remember to ask how, what, when, where and why questions, rather than questions that require 'Yes' or 'No' as answers.

10 simple things you could do to raise your own self-esteem

Learn new things that challenge you

Balance your cheque book regularly

Sift through your wardrobe and pass on clothes that no longer fit or suit you

Sort through your cupboards and desk and throw out what is no longer relevant

Exercise regularly

Write letters or make telephone calls that you have been promising yourself that you will do for ages

Stop saying you will do things that you are not going to attend to immediately

Complete unfinished business

Clear up broken agreements

Clean your car — and keep it like that

Learn to converse in questions, not to interrogate but to use a wide variety of creative resources and expand your way of interacting with the world around you.

Ask more questions than you give answers. In fact, give up thinking that you have to have answers. There probably are none.

Learn to ask better and better questions — and then be sure you listen. This is not the time to display how wise and clever you are. Teach young people to develop inquiring, probing minds and to ask better and better questions. Show them how to seek information about their enquiries.

We often meet teenagers who are *surprised* that some adults are actually interested in what they think. The most street-wise and hardened teenagers have often warmed to these adults.

Use family resources. Review your extended family. Who could help you and your children? Who could you and your children help? Have another look at the section on blended families in this book.

Share with friends. Support each other and realise the value in this. Notice, however, if your friends are supporting you to be less than you can be. Is this healthy? Are they colluding with you to keep you hooked into being a victim, for instance? Perhaps they are inviting you to keep telling your 'poor me' stories and sympathising, instead of asking you to consider more powerful options.

Meet your children's friends' parents. Ask them if they agree about some rules, such as the time to be home on Saturday nights and week nights. Ask them to support you in sticking to these rules.

Spend time with your partner. Find time to be with your partner alone, without the children. Try to arrange something definite once a week or a weekend occasionally. Even ten minutes talking quietly each evening might be the break you need.

> *Literature is mostly about having sex and not much about having children: life is the other way around.*
>
>
>
> **David Lodge**

Use community resources. Explore what's out there in your community: karate classes, guides, scouts, team sports, neighbourhood houses, community care centres, health centres, citizens advice bureaux. What else is there?

Make sure you have a source of spiritual sustenance. It's worth shopping around, exploring, visiting different

> *Love, Hope, and Self-esteem,*
> *like clouds depart*
> *And come, for some uncertain*
> *moments lent.*

Percy Bysshe Shelley

groups and people and making enquiries until you find something that enriches and strengthens your inner life. Something that you can believe in with the familiar, comfortable feeling that you have come home.

Meditation has been a tried and true must for both of us through many challenging periods and over a long period of time.

Seek help from professionals when necessary. It is important to find someone who will just listen and can be used as a sounding board, with whom you can bounce ideas around, who won't shower you with 'You should …' and 'You must …'.

Mostly you will resolve the issues in your own mind as you talk. Trust yourself to do this.

Be careful of people who leave you feeling inadequate.

Remember that some very worthwhile, resourceful and creative human beings have been thoroughly obnoxious at some time in their teens. It's healthy for teenagers to feel a bit rebellious at times. Most do and most turn out alright in the end.

Congratulate yourself frequently on how well you are doing.

Be kind to yourself. You are only able to be kind to anyone else while you are feeling kindly towards yourself.

When all else fails, do two things: Go for a long, energetic walk — or run. Then lock yourself in the bathroom and have a bath with a few drops of essential lavender oil in it, by candlelight. Turn on your favourite music, and have faith that all will be OK in the long run.

Through our journey we have both come to realise that the bottom line for all of us is to be able to give and receive love.

It takes a whole village to raise a child.

♥

Guy A. Zona

21

When you need support, get it!

Resource File

There has never been more information about how to cope, how to relate, how to communicate. Make education in these areas a priority. Develop your own Resource File, with what's available to you – in your local community, on the telephone, by mail order. Remember that prevention is always better than cure, so consider doing a course on parenting, get involved in a sport with your kids, and find out what your local community has to offer your family, so that you can enjoy your teenagers.

The following list should help get you started.

PARENTING

Good sources of information regarding the many services, self-help groups etc. are the departments of Health and Community Services in each state (the official name of these government departments vary slightly from state to state – check your phone book). They are able to offer advice or referral to other groups, on a whole range of parenting issues and information, such as assertive parenting, violence in the family, single parent families, step families, adoption etc.

Parent Effectiveness Training (P.E.T.) is an example of the type of course available for parents to learn skills. The Australian Council for Educational Research has information on parenting skills and resources. Check your phone book for state contacts.

Parent support groups/help lines

VIC
Parents Anonymous
156 Collins Street
Melbourne (03) 9654 4654

NSW
The Parents Support Network
(02) 832 1242

QLD
Parenting Advice and Information
Ph (07) 224 7588

SA
Parents Support Group
(08) 374 1809

WA
Parent Information and Resource Service
Ph (09) 272 1444, 008 807 648
Parent Help Centre
Ph (09) 272 1466, 008 807 648

TAS
Parenting Centre, Newtown
Ph (002) 33 2700, 1800 808 178
Family Support Service
Ph (002) 29 4602

NT
Community Care Centre
Ph (089) 89 2876

ACT
Parent Support Service
Ph (06) 247 0519

Relationships Australia

Relationships Australia is a national organisation offering relationship services through counselling, education and mediation. Courses include 'Parenting Adolescents', 'Growing Together – Parents and Kids' and 'Loneliness and Teenagers'.

VIC
(03) 9853 5354

WA
(09) 470 5109

NSW
(02) 418 8800

TAS
(002) 236 041

QLD
(07) 839 9144

NT
(089) 816 676

SA
(08) 223 4566

ACT
(062) 81 3600

Toughlove

Toughlove is a non-profit, self-help program for parents troubled by teenage behaviour. Toughlove is not a parenting program – it is a crisis intervention programme. Toughlove groups are run by parents and provide an extended family of caring adults. It offers a solution for families who are being torn apart by unacceptable adolescent behaviour.

Information
All states
Margaret Gardner
Toughlove
c/ Relationships Australia
55 Hutt Street
Adelaide 5000
Ph (08) 223 4566
Fax (08) 232 2898

SAFE SEX & FAMILY PLANNING

If you don't feel comfortable giving your kids the information they need – or they don't feel comfortable hearing it from you – make sure they get the information they need *somehow*. Invest in some good books (see our book list following), get some up-to-date brochures, or find someone they can talk to. If they don't want to go in to one of the Clinics, they can often ring.

Family Planning Clinics' range of services in most states includes contraceptive information and supplies, testing and where necessary treatment of sexually transmitted diseases (STD). There are counselling services for relationships, sexual abuse, family hassles, stressing out with school, and more. Ring the Clinic in your state and find out what they have to offer.

VIC
Action Centre, Family Planning Victoria
(This is especially geared to young people.)
277 Flinders Lane
Melbourne 3000
Ph (03) 9654 4766
1800 013 952

NSW
Family Planning Association
328-336 Liverpool Road
Ashfield 2131
Ph (02) 716 6099

QLD
Family Planning Association
100 Alfred Street
Fortitude Valley 4006
Ph (07) 252 5151

SA
Family Planning Association
17 Phillips Street
Kensington 5068
Ph (08) 31 5177

WA
Family Planning Association
70 Roe Street
Northbridge 6865
Ph (09) 227 6177, toll free 1800 19 8205

TAS
Family Planning Association
73 Federal Street
North Hobart 7002
Ph (002) 34 7200, toll free 1800 00 7119

NT
Family Planning Association
Shop 11, Rapid Creek Shopping Centre
Rapid Creek 0810
Ph (089) 48 0144, toll free (008) 19 3121, fax (089) 480 626

ACT
Family Planning Association
Health Promotion Centre
Childers Street
Canberra 2600
Ph (06) 247 3077

ALCOHOL & DRUG INFORMATION

NATIONAL
Information
Australian Drug Foundation
PO Box 529
South Melbourne 3205
Ph (03) 690 6000
or (0055) 222 99

VIC
Counselling and referral
Ph (03) 416 1818 or
toll free outside Melbourne 1800 136 385

NSW
Information
CEIDA (Centre for Education and Information on Drugs
and Alcohol
Ph (02) 818 5222/0444
Counselling and referral
St Vincent's Hospital
Victoria Street
Darlinghurst 2010
Ph (02) 339 1111 or
toll free outside Sydney 1800 422 599

QLD
Information
'Biala' Alcohol and Drug Dependency Service
Ph (07) 236 2400
Counselling and referral
Ph (07) 236 2414 or
toll free outside Brisbane (008) 177 833

SA
Information
Drug and Alcohol Services Council
3/161 Greenhill Road
Parkside 5063
Ph (08) 274 3333

Counselling and referral
Phone toll free 13 1340

WA
Information
WA Alcohol and Drug Authority
7 Field Street
Mount Lawley
Ph (09) 370 0333 or
toll free outside Perth 1800 198 024

TAS
Information
Alcohol and Drug Service
Ph Hobart (002) 784 111, north Launceston (003) 327 167
north west Tas (004) 255 511 also Launceston (003) 374 210

Counselling and referral
Ph (002) 282 880 or toll free 1800 811 994

NT
Information
Early Intervention Unit
Department of Health and Community Services
Ph (089) 22 8888

Counselling and referral
Ph (089) 818 030

ACT
Information
Alcohol and other Drug Council of Australia
Ph (06) 281 0686

Counselling and referral
Ph (06) 205 1323 — Drug & Alcohol Department
Ph (06) 205 1338 — Counselling

DRUG REHABILITATION

Odyssey House is a drug-free, in-residence, therapeu
munity for the treatment of the drug abuser. It has reside
in Victoria and New South Wales, but takes in people from
all over Australia.

VIC
Odyssey House
The Odyssey Community Involvement Centre
173 Greville Street Prahran Vic 3181
Ph (03) 510 5394

NSW
The Odyssey Community Involvement Centre
431 Elizabeth Street
Surry Hills NSW 2010
Ph (02) 281 5144

VIC
Windana
Windana's Drug Rehabilitation programme is run at a
residence in St Kilda and a farm at Pakenham.
88 Alma Road
St Kilda Vic 3182
Ph 9529 7955

SA
The Woolshed
P.O. Box 84
Ashbourne 5157
Ph (085) 366 002

Insight

Insight runs programmes in all states for those who want to
improve their life skills in the area of relationships, work,

…ic com-
…nces

…e support, get it!

143

…ishes to have more, do more
…t seminars are very practical,
…l yet simple techniques that
…ly lives. There are courses for
…n. The Insight seminars have
…with some of the kids from

…
All states
12 Carlotta Street
Artarmon 2065
Ph (02) 439 1488
or 1800 677 488

SEEK International

SEEK conducts self-esteem and accelerated learning programmes for primary children, teenagers, parents, teachers
and schools. Courses cover self-esteem, confidence, motiva-
tion, goal setting, relationships, communication skills, easy
learning strategies and more. Courses are held in
Melbourne, Sydney and Brisbane

Information
All states
PO Box 6066 Doncaster MDC
Vic 3108
Ph (03) 9761 925, (03) 9840 2736
1800 679 326

Education for Life

Human Resource Consultants specialising in personal and
professional development of adults and teenagers.
Seminars are run in most states.

Information
All states
Education for Life Pty Ltd
4/188 Longueville Rd
Lane Cove 2066
Ph (02) 418 6696
Fax (02) 418 8668

Born to be Free

Born to Be Free runs two-day seminars to help clear people of their negative childhood conditioning and emotions, helping create permanent confidence and self-esteem. Seminars are held in all states for adults and teenagers.

Information
All states
Ph (03) 9804 7353

Breaking the Cycle

This organisation conducts programs for long term unemployed and/or homeless youth between the ages of 15 and 21. The program involves a wilderness challenge to build self-esteem and teamwork and to promote a positive attitude to work and life. Programs are run nationally.

VIC
Ph (03) 9699 3164, Fax (03) 9696 9539

NSW
Ph 0411 102 232 (mobile)

QLD
Ph (07) 236 3465
Fax (07) 236 4246

The Inner Child

'Twenty Twenty Learning' run inner child workshops that help people re-discover the child within themselves, enabling them to achieve a greater level of freedom, personal power and creativity. The workshops help people to create and maintain loving relationships, to let go of parental influence and beliefs that can sabotage their relationships with their own children. Workshops are held in most states.

Information
All states
Dick Crompton
Twenty Twenty Learning
PO Box 451 Cammeray NSW 2062
Ph (02) 231 4591 or
toll free 1800 808 707

Light Unlimited Productions

Sherrill and James Sellman, who set up the group, are psychotherapists, seminar leaders and trainers. They assist people to easily and quickly resolve long-standing personal limitations. Their work includes resolving trauma and abuse, relationship difficulties, low self-esteem and health problems.

VIC
Sherrill & James Sellman
PO Box 184 East Kew 3102
Ph (03) 9810 9591
Fax (03) 9859 7062

NSW
Quentin Watts (02) 810 6100
Michael Adamedes (02) 557 3399

WA
Kate Faraday (09) 310 1884

SA
Margaret Johnson (08) 370 9323
Julie Way (08) 439 162
Annie O'Grady (08) 391 2594

NLP (Neuro Linguistic Programming)

NLP is a way of studying how we think. Practical skills in it enable parents to better understand their teenagers, and importantly, be understood. It can help parents to maintain and enhance their relationships, even under stressful circumstances.

International NLP Trainers Association
All states, Ph (03) 9826 6944
All states, Fax (03) 9826 8235

Integrated Learning –
Victoria and WA
Ph (03) 9787 5050
Fax (03) 9787 3460

Inform Training and Research P/L
NSW
Ph (02) 211 1300
Fax (02) 211 1095

Further Learning

If you are interested in courses and seminars that expand your own education and that of your teenagers, the following would be a good starting point. For information in all states:

Sales Pursuit Results Pty Ltd
Ian Low
Ph (02) 281 8177
toll free 1800 244 388

Jerry Speiser
Onboard Communications
Ph (03) 9877 9855

Wilson Jordan Group
Ph (03) 9699 6555

GRIEF

Compassionate Friends
This group offers bereaved parent support and
information.

VIC
Bereaved Parent Centre
Ph (03) 9882 33 55
toll free 1 800 641 091

NSW
Drop In Centre
Ph (02) 233 3731
toll free 1 800 671 621

QLD
The Compassionate Friends
Ph (07) 359 8007

SA
Drop In Centre
Ph (08) 294 6700

WA
Drop In Centre
Ph (09) 227 5698

TAS
Central Tas Ph (002) 55 2145
Southern Tas (002) 29 4654
Northern Tas (003) 44 4955

NT
Ph (089) 27 8416
(089) 72 3198

ACT
Ph (06) 286 6134

SPORT

It's worth trying to get your kids involved in sport. Check out what's available through local community centres, which often have sport training and courses at a much cheaper rate than private tuition.

Sportscamp

Sportscamp runs residential camp programmes for 11 to 15 year old boys and girls from all backgrounds. It encourages sporting ability as well as creating an environment where young people learn the value of teamwork, leadership and respecting the rights and needs of all individuals.

466 Punt Road
South Yarra 3141
Vic Ph (03) 9820 8407
Fax (03) 9866 6717

Outward Bound

Outward Bound is a non-profit organisation specialising in adventure-based education for 12 to 70 year olds. Courses are conducted in various locations and activities include abseiling, rock climbing, canoeing, rafting, navigating and bush cooking. The purpose is to promote self-confidence, self-reliance and an appreciation of your abilities and of others.

VIC
(03) 9873 1031

SA
Ph (08) 297 0497

NSW
(02) 261 2200
or toll free 1800 267 999

WA
(09) 221 4252

BODY IMAGE

Anorexia nervosa and bulimia can cause severe physical damage to the body and anyone suffering from either of these conditions needs professional help. There are also some very good books on these subjects, as well as body image.

VIC
Anorexia and Bulimia Nervosa Foundation of Vic
1513 High Street
Glen Iris Vic 3146
Ph (03) 9885 0318

NSW
Northside Clinic (private) (02) 439 6866
Westmead Hospital (public) (02) 633 6686

QLD
Bulimia Anorexia Nervosa Support Group
c/ Queensland Assoc. of Mental Health
Friendship House
20 Balfour Street
Newfarm
Ph (07) 358 4988

SA
Anorexia Nervosa and Bulimia Association
35 Fullarton Road
Kent Town 5067
Ph (08) 362 6772, 1800 182 079

WA
Bulimia and Anorexia Nervosa Group
PO Box 794
Nedlands 6009
(09) 474 2598

ACT
ACT Anorexia and Bulimia Support Group
PO Box 773
Woden ACT 2606
Ph (06) 286 3941

EDUCATION

Check the State Education Departments for community and alternative schools. The Association of Independent Schools publish lists of private schools including alternative schools with their philosophies.

Association of Independent Schools

VIC
(03) 9826 6011

WA
(09) 244 2788

NSW
(02) 299 2845

TAS
(003) 34 1908

QLD
(07) 839 2122

NT
(089) 723 9286

SA
(08) 373 0755

ACT
(06) 241 2429

EMERGENCY COUNSELLING

These are 24-hour counselling and emergency lines. Some states have a special 'Youthline'. Check your phone book.

VIC
Lifeline statewide Ph 13 1114
or Melbourne (03) 9662 1000

NSW
Lifeline statewide Ph 13 1114
or Sydney (02) 281 8588

QLD
Lifeline statewide Ph 13 1114
or Brisbane (07) 252 7086

SA
Lifeline statewide Ph 13 1114
or Adelaide (08) 212 3444

WA
Samaritans Ph (09) 381 5555
or toll free 1800 19 8313

TAS
Lifeline statewide Ph 13 1114

NT
Crisis Line Ph (089) 819 227
or toll free 1800 01 9116

ACT
Lifeline statewide Ph 13 1114
or Canberra (06) 257 1111

Some books we have found very helpful

PARENTING

THE SECRET OF HAPPY CHILDREN, Steve Biddulph, Bay Books, Sydney, 1994

PARENTING TEENAGERS IN THE 1990s, Bob Dyers, ACER, Australia, 1992

PARENT EFFECTIVENESS TRAINING, Gordon Thomas, Plume, New York, 1970

FIGHT-FREE FAMILIES, Dr Janet Hall, Lothian Books, 1994

CONFIDENT CHILDREN A Parent's Guide to Helping Children Feel Good About Themselves, Gael Lindenfield, Thorsons, 1994

PARENTING FOR EVERYONE Meeting the Challenge, Vijayuadev Yodendra, The Total Health and Education Centre for Learning, Warwick, 1989

TOUGHLOVE, Phyllis and David Yorke and Ted Watchel, Bantam Books, 1992

CONFLICT/ANGER

EVERYONE CAN WIN How to Resolve Conflict, Helena Cornelius and Shoshana Faire, Simon and Schuster, Australia, 1994

MANAGING ANGER Positive Strategies for Dealing with Difficult Emotions, Gael Lindenfield, Thorsons, 1993

HEALTH: MIND & BODY

QUANTUM HEALING Exploring the Frontiers of Mind/Body Medicine, Deepak Chopra, Bantam New Age Books, 1990

REAL GORGEOUS The Truth about Body and Beauty, Kaz Cooke, Allen & Unwin, Australia, 1994

THE NEW PRIMAL SCREAM Primal Therapy Twenty Years On Dr Arthur Janou, Abacus, 1993

HEALING THE SHAME THAT BINDS YOU, John Bradshaw, Health Communications, USA, 1989

CREATING LOVE, John Bradshaw, Health Communications, USA, 1990

ONE MINUTE SELF-ESTEEM, Candy Semigran, Insight Publishing, 1988

SPIRITUAL

REFLECTIONS IN THE LIGHT, Shakti Gawain, New World Library, California, 1988

FOCUS ON THE POSITIVE & SELF-DEVELOPMENT

MANHOOD, Steve Biddulph, Bay Books, Sydney, 1994

THE 7 HABITS OF HIGHLY EFFECTIVE PEOPLE, Stephen R Covey, Simon and Schuster, New York, 1989

QUANTUM LEARNING, Bobby de Porter, Dell Publishing, New York, 1992

FEEL THE FEAR AND DO IT ANYWAY How to Turn Your Fear and Indecision into Confidence and Action, Susan Jeffers, Arrow, 1987

YOU CAN'T AFFORD THE LUXURY OF A NEGATIVE THOUGHT, John-Roger and Peter McWilliams, Thorsons, 1991

YOU JUST DON'T UNDERSTAND, Deborah Tannen, Random House, 1991

AN ACTION PLAN FOR YOUR INNER CHILD, Parenting Each Other, Laurie Weiss, Health Communications, USA, 1991

YOU CAN HAVE IT ALL, Arnold M Patent, Celebration Publishing, 1991

HEART OF THE MIND Engaging your inner power to change with Neuro Linguistic Programming, Connirae and Steve Andreas, Real People Press, Utah, 1989

WHY DON'T PEOPLE LISTEN Solving the Communication Problem, Hugh McKay, Pan Australia, 1994

AWAKEN THE GIANT WITHIN How to Take Immediate Control of Your Mental, Emotional, Physical and Financial Destiny, Anthony Robbins, Fireside Books, New York, 1991

IF YOU WANT TO BE RICH AND HAPPY DON'T GO TO SCHOOL Robert Kiyosaki, Excellerated Learning Publishing, 1991

RELATIONSHIPS

HOW'S YOUR LOVE LIFE, Merry Watson, Hale and Iremonger, Sydney

LOVNG RELATIONSHIPS, Sandra Ray, Celestial Arts Publishing, Berkeley, 1992

WOMEN WHO RUN WITH THE WOLVES Contacting the Power of the Wild Woman, Clarissa Pinkola Estés, Rider, USA, 1993

DREAMS

DREAM POWER, Ann Faraday, Berkeley Books, New York, 1981

CREATIVE DREAMING, Patricia Garfield, Ballantine Books, New York, 1976

ADOPTION

STEPS UP THE MOUNTAIN: The story of the DeBolt family, J. B. Lippincott Company, Philadelphia

DEATH/GRIEF

HOW TO SURVIVE THE LOSS OF A LOVE, M Colgrove, H Bloomfield and P McWilliams, Bantam, 1991

DEATH: THE FINAL STAGE OF GROWTH, Elisabeth Kubler-Ross, Prentice-Hall, New Jersey 1975

SEX EDUCATION

THE MODERN GIRLS' GUIDE TO SAFE SEX, Kaz Cooke, McPhee Gribble, Melbourne, 1993

TAUGHT NOT CAUGHT Self Esteem in Sex Education, Clarity Collective, Globe Press, 1991

LEAN ON ME, Tom Roxburgh and the Lean On Me Sexual Assault Support Group, Goulburn Valley Centre Against Sexual Assault, Shepparton, 1991

GOOD READING FOR YOUNG PEOPLE

THE 1995 WHAT COLOR IS YOUR PARACHUTE, Richard Nelson Bolles, Ten Speed Press, California, 1995

WAY OF THE PEACEFUL WARRIOR, Dan Millman, H. J. Kramer, 1984

YOU CAN HEAL YOUR LIFE, Louise Hay, Specialist Publications, Sydney, 1994

IT COULD BE DIFFERENT A Self-Help Book for Teenagers, Amrita Hobbs, Harmond Holidays, Australia, 1991

SUPER STUDY A New Age Study Guide, John Wade, Dellasta, Melbourne, 1990

THE RICHEST MAN IN BABYLON, George S Clason, Penguin Books, Australia, 1992

THE CREATIVE COMPANION, How to free your creative spirit, Sark, Celestial Arts, Berkeley, 1991

THE CELESTINE PROPHECY, James Redfield, Bantam, Australia, 1994

JONATHON LIVINGSTONE SEAGULL, Richard Bach, Harper Collins, London, 1994

Source of quotes

The authors and publisher wish to acknowledge and thank the following for quotes reproduced: p 18 *Happiness is a Choice*, Barry Neil Kaufman (Ballantyne Books, New York); p 22 *Creative Dreaming* Patricia Garfield (Ballantyne Books, New York); p 36 Deepak Chopra interview with Anthony Robbins (Deepak Chopra's own books are published by Crown Publishers, USA); p 48 Hugh Mackay, interview with Kate Legge (c. *The Australian Magazine*); p 50 *Five Freedoms* poster Virginia Satir (Celestial Arts, California); p 54 Helen Kromer, Insight Training Seminar book; p 62 & p 96 *You Can't Afford the Luxury of a Negative Thought* John-Roger & Peter McWilliams (Prelude Press, 1988); p 69 *Why Don't People Listen* Hugh Mackay (Pan Macmillan Australia Pty Ltd, copyright Hugh Mackay, 1994); p 71 *The Handbook to Higher Consciousness* Ken Keyes, Jr (Living Love Publications, Oregon, 1975); p 90 Shakti Gawain, *Living in the Light* (New World Library, USA); p 100 *Perspectives on a Grafted Tree* Fleur Conkling Heylinger (Perspectives Press, USA); p 110 *Love is Letting Go of Fear*, Gerald G Jampolsky (Celestial Arts, Berkeley, USA, 1979); p 114 *Return to Love* Marianne Williamson (Harper Collins, USA); p 122 Sir J Lubbock, quoted on a Celestial Seasonings tea packet; p 131 David Lodge, desk diary (Reed Consumer Books, UK).